BASIC ENGLISH SKILLS

BASIC ENGLISH SKILLS

PAT HORNE & MIKE OUZMAN

Hodder & Stoughton

A MEMBER OF THE HODDER HEADLINE GROUP

British Library Cataloguing in Publication Data

Home, Pat
  Basic English Skills
  Student's book
  1. English language — Grammar — 1950–
  I. Title II. Ouzman, Mike
  428   PE112

ISBN 0 340 38951 6

First published 1987
Impression number   14 13 12 11 10 9 8 7 6
Year   1999 1998 1997 1996 1995 1994

Copyright © 1987 Pat Home and Mike Ouzman

Printed in Great Britain for Hodder & Stoughton Educational, a divisional of Hodder Headline Plc, 338 Euston Road, London NW1 3BH by The Bath Press, Lower Bristol Road, Bath

Contents

Preface

This book aims to provide instruction in techniques and to give practice in basic English skills.

A number of exercises have been devised to help students gain experience of listening, understanding, responding to the spoken word, selecting key information and indexing it, and completing forms and letters from given information to meet a number of everyday situations.

The book is suitable for preparing students for the AEB Basic English examination, and is useful for aspects of the City and Guilds Communication Skills and CPVE communication work. It could also be extremely useful for EFL courses.

The book is designed to be used in the classroom in conjunction with the Teachers' Book which contains listening passages, dictation passages, and mark schemes.

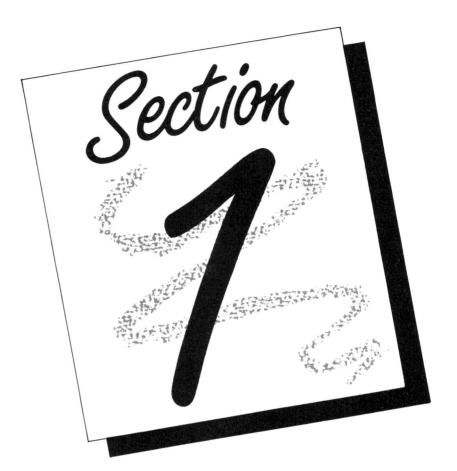

Section

1

Listening skills

One of the most useful skills anyone can develop for communication at work is the ability to listen, remember and respond.

Most of us, however, can't remember everything we hear, even after a short lapse of time. Psychologists have shown that we all have different types of memory for different tasks, and we remember facts selectively. Some facts are easier to remember, too.

Any interruptions, any interference, can make us forget what we heard, and we can lose half of what we learnt within an hour!

So a message that says this

> Your grandmother telephoned to say that she'll
> be arriving at Victoria railway station at
> 8.30 tonight but don't get worried because she'll
> get a taxi home all right.

Message 1

can become this   or this

> Grandmother telephoned
> arriving Victoria
> railway station 8.30
> tonight but she'll
> get a taxi home.

Message 2

> Your mother telephoned to
> say at station tonight but
> worried because she'll taxi
> home.

Message 3

Add the fact that **most people fill in the gaps** from their imagination and *Message 3* becomes this

> Your mother *has just* telephoned *from a* station
> *somewhere* to say *she'll be back home* tonight
> *but she's very* worried because *she's got no money
> and* she'll *not be able to take a* taxi home *if
> she's not got the fare.*

Message 4

If you think this is far-fetched, just try passing a message around the class and seeing what happens to it. This is the process of **distortion.**

What can we do about distortion? Well, we can try to concentrate on just the **key facts** (as in *Message 2*). And we can **write them down** as we hear them.

If we write them down, we are learning them twice, once through our ears and a second time through our eyes. The written message is more permanent, and jogs our memory anyway.

Finally, we can **practice the skills**, because practice makes perfect — or at least, it helps us improve. This is what this section is all about.

Situation 1: Answer-phone

When you get into work in the morning, there is a message already recorded on the Answer-phone tape. Listen to it as it is read to you by your teacher, and then answer the questions that will be read. The message and the questions will be read only once. It would be a good idea to take notes as you listen.

Situation 2: Railway-station anouncement

You will listen to a message which was given over the loudspeaker at a railway station. Then answer the questions that will be read to you. Remember to take notes. You will hear the announcement and the questions only once.

Situation 3: A message at the theatre

You go on a trip to the theatre with your school or college. During the interval a message is announced from the stage.

Listen to the message. Then answer the questions about it. You will hear the message and the questions only once.

Situation 4: TV extract

'Spotlight on Crime' is a regional television programme. Police officers ask members of the public to help track down criminals or to trace stolen goods.

Listen to the extract from the programme. Then answer the questions about it. You will hear the extract and the questions only once.

Situation 5: Telephone message

You work part-time in a local grocery shop. Your boss has gone to the warehouse to fetch some more stock when the telephone rings.

Listen to the message. Then answer the questions about it. You will hear the message and the questions only once.

Situation 6: Local radio message

On your local radio station there is a 'News and Views' programme. Sometimes descriptions of property that has been lost or stolen are given, in case a member of the public has seen it.

   Listen to the message about an item of lost property. Then answer the questions about it. You will hear the message and the questions only once.

Situation 7: Hotel loudspeaker announcements

You work in a large hotel which lets out rooms for meetings and conferences. The hotel has a loudspeaker system.

   Listen to the announcements from the loudspeakers. Then answer the questions about them. You will hear the announcements and the questions only once.

Situation 8: Police message

You are listening to music on the radio when the following police message is given.

   Listen to the message. Then answer the questions about it. You will hear the message and the questions only once.

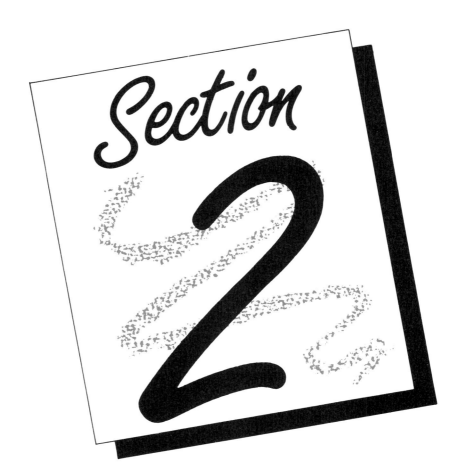

Section

2

Selecting key information

Sometimes you have to take out a very small amount of information from a huge mass. Sometimes *only part* of it is relevant to you. Sometimes a lot of it is waffle.

The two skills you need here are   **SUMMARY**

and   **SELECTION OF KEY INFORMATION**

To take summary first:

Summary is where you take the general idea and 'sum it up'. Sometimes you can find one word to take the place of half-a-dozen.
For example,

Paper clips Envelopes Writing paper Drawing pins Staples	=	Stationery

Cars Lorries Buses Coaches Bikes	=	Transport

Sometimes a long paragraph can be reduced to about a dozen words.
For example,

It is important to realise that safety at work is everyone's concern — the safety representatives, the managers and the supervisors, and all the employees — all have their part to play in keeping the workplace a safe place	=	Everyone has a part to play in safety at work. Everyone has some responsibility for safety

Take the reading passage from Answer-phone (Section 1, Situation 1) as an example.

What you **actually heard** was this

Message 1 this is Dave Stone Regional Manager for the North Region ■ could you please pass this message on to Mrs Williams the Branch Manager or her assistant if she is not in ■ I have to go to Birmingham on Thursday for a conference so I would like to drop in and see you ■ I shall probably be at your branch about one o'clock or one thirty at the latest ■ I have some publicity material to pass on to you and it is easier to explain it than to post it ■ if it is inconvenient to call please telephone me before nine thirty on my home telephone number Leeds 03 9029 ■ thank you ■

A **summary** would look something like this

Message 2 Message for Mrs Williams/assistant Branch Manager: The Regional Manager telephoned. He will be calling in at our Branch about one o'clock to one-thirty to pass on some publicity material. Call him at home before 9.30 (Leeds 03-9029), if that is inconvenient for you.

So **Summary** sometimes has an important part to play in getting to the heart of a message.

However, often it is more important just to recognise the **KEY INFORMATION** in a passage. '**Key information**' is the most important information (just as a key worker is someone who is vital to the firm).

Look back at *Message 1* again. If you just selected the **key information**, you would concentrate on names, dates, places, positions, reasons, explanations — what someone is doing, why they are doing it. So **key information notes** would look like this:

Message 3 Dave Stone — Regional Manager — North Message for — Mrs Williams or her assistant Going to Birmingham — Thursday (conference). Calling here 1 o'clock (1.30 latest) – publicity material for you. Telephone — before 9.30 if inconvenient at Leeds 03-9029 (home number)

In both Messages 2 and 3, a lot of unnecessary words are left out. You generally have to have both skills for taking messages. But picking the key information — the important details — is perhaps more important. Look at Message 3. It gives names, it gives times and dates, it gives two places ('Birmingham' and 'here'), and it gives the important explanations (about the conference and the publicity material).

To help practise the skills of summary and selection of key information, all the following situations will have the questions printed out for you.

Situation 9: First day at work

You will hear a talk that was originally given by a girl called Helen about her first day at work. You will hear the talk twice. You should make notes as you listen. It is quite a long talk, and it may be shortened. Whether you hear the short version or the longer one, without notes it is very likely that you will forget some of the key points, even if you try to write all the answers down as you listen.

Of course you can write notes and answers at any time during the two readings. Your notes, however, will not be marked. A few minutes will be given at the end of the second reading for you to write your answers.

In particular, try to get the names right. Give the title (Mr, Mrs/Miss/Ms), if it is given. Notice that several questions require two answers. Question 2 *tells* you two examples are needed. But you have to look at the questions to realise that two answers are needed for questions 4 and 7, for example.

Sometimes, though not often, you might have a choice of what to put down (question 2 is an easy one in that respect). Generally, however, there are only two possible answers to an (a) and (b) question, so listen carefully for the second one.

FIRST DAY AT WORK

You will hear a talk read to you that was originally given by a girl called Helen about her first day at work. You will hear the talk twice. You should make notes as you listen, because it is quite a long passage. Study the questions first to get an idea of what to look for. You may write your answers at any time.

1. Who was the person Helen was supposed to report to?
   .... (1 mark)

2. Give *two* details of the personal appearance of this person.
   (a) .... (1 mark)
   (b) .... (1 mark)

3. Who was Mandy?
   .... (1 mark)

4. What sort of work had Helen done before?
   (a) .... (1 mark)
   (b) .... (1 mark)

5. What was the first thing Helen and Mandy had to do in the upstairs office?
   .... (1 mark)

6. What did Helen promise herself that she would do when she got her uniform?
   .... (1 mark)

7. Why did the sales assistants have to leave the note outside the till drawer whilst they gave change?
   (a) .... (1 mark)
   (b) .... (1 mark)

***

8. Who did Mandy go to work with on a counter?
   .... (1 mark)

9. Who did Helen go to work with on a counter?
   .... (1 mark)

10. What did Mandy sell on her counter?
    .... (1 mark)

11. Who was 'Aunty'?
    .... (1 mark)

12. In which two places was spare stock kept?
    (a) .... (1 mark)
    (b) .... (1 mark)

13. What did Helen and her fellow-worker have to do when not serving customers or fetching stock?
    .... (1 mark)

14. Why did they have to do this so much?
    .... (1 mark)

15. Who were obviously the best customers?
    .... (1 mark)

16. Why was that so strange?
    .... (1 mark)

17. Why was it hardly worth opening the store in winter?
    .... (1 mark)

18. How can we tell that the cook was obviously a 'very jolly lady'?
    (a) .... (1 mark)
    (b) .... (1 mark)

19. Why did Helen drink unsweetened tea?
    .... (1 mark)

20. How did Helen feel after serving several customers?
    .... (1 mark)

Situation 10: Community service

This situation was first given as a talk by an outside speaker to a group of Fifth and Sixth Formers. One morning a week they did a Community Service project. During that time they would do a number of things, such as helping with young children, or the handicapped, or — as in this case — helping with old people. The speaker is from the Home Help Service.

You will hear the talk twice. You should make notes as you listen. These notes will not be marked. Study the questions before listening to the talk, so you know what to listen for.

In particular, listen carefully for the answer to question 10: there are two answers to it, and the question is quite tricky. Notice the word **not** in question 11, too. The final tricky question is question 19, which needs a very full, quite long answer: don't give just half the answer; there are no half-marks.

COMMUNITY SERVICE

You will hear a talk given by a speaker from the Home Help Service. You will hear the talk twice. You should make notes as you listen. These notes will not be marked. You may write your answers at any time. At the end of the second reading you will have four minutes to complete your answers.

1. What is the speaker's name?
   .... (1 mark)

2. What is the speaker's job?
   .... (1 mark)

3. How often will you be working?
   .... (1 mark)

4. What hours will you work?
   .... (1 mark)

5. When will you first visit the old lady or gentleman?
   .... (1 mark)

6. Why will you be given an official name badge and a Voluntary Home Help card?
   .... (1 mark)

7. On what day will the old people have their Home Helps?
   .... (1 mark)

8. On what day will you be visiting them?
   .... (1 mark)

9. Being a Home Help is not being a 'Mrs Mop'. What is the job of a Home Help more like?
   .... (1 mark)

10. Apart from talking to the old people, what other work might you be asked to do?

    (a) .... (1 mark)

    (b) .... (1 mark)

11. What work should you *not* have to do?

    .... (1 mark)

12. Why is the most important part of the work talking to the old people?

    .... (1 mark)

13. Why must the Home Help card be signed?

    .... (1 mark)

14. What should you get the old person to do if he or she cannot write?

    .... (1 mark)

15. Why can't some of the old people write?

    .... (1 mark)

16. For how long will you go to the same old person before you get a change?

    .... (1 mark)

17. Why do Home Helps get a change every so often?

    .... (1 mark)

18. What do the Home Help Service do with the odd bad case?

    .... (1 mark)

19. What should you do if you get a problem?

    .... (1 mark)

Situation 11: Hospital work experience

You will hear a talk by someone who has done some work experience in a local hospital. Although the speaker does not actually say so, she is obviously female and probably still at school or at college. However, it is quite likely that similar tasks are done by boys in that area.

You will hear the talk twice. You should make notes as you listen because some of the information is quite detailed and you need to select the relevant details. These notes will not be marked.

There are two possible answers for question 2, and three possible answers for questions 6 and 16. You need put down only *one* of them.

However, for questions 7 and 13, you are *asked* for two answers and both are needed. Full answers are needed to questions 9 and 14.

Study the questions before listening to the talk, so you know what to listen for.

HOSPITAL WORK EXPERIENCE
You will hear a talk given by a student who has done some work experience in a local hospital. You will hear the talk twice. You should make notes as you listen. These notes will not be marked. You may write your answers at any time. At the end of the second reading you will have four minutes to complete your answers.

1. What was the job that the speaker had been doing for work experience?
   ………………………………………………………………………… (1 mark)

2. Why did the speaker like the job?
   ………………………………………………………………………… (1 mark)

3. How old was the speaker when she had been in a hospital before?
   ………………………………………………………………………… (1 mark)

4. What had she been in hospital for?
   ………………………………………………………………………… (1 mark)

5. What was the name of the ward where the girl was working?
   ………………………………………………………………………… (1 mark)

6. What kind of ward was it?
   ………………………………………………………………………… (1 mark)

7. Give two details of the Ward Sister's appearance.
   (a) ……………………………………………………………………… (1 mark)
   (b) ……………………………………………………………………… (1 mark)

8. At what time did the girl start work?
   ………………………………………………………………………… (1 mark)

9. What was her first task?
   ………………………………………………………………………… (1 mark)

10. Why did taking the fresh water out take such a long time?
   ………………………………………………………………………… (1 mark)

11. What time did the post come at?
   ………………………………………………………………………… (1 mark)

12. Who brought the post?
   ………………………………………………………………………… (1 mark)

13. The speaker had to take messages to other parts of the hospital. What examples did she give?
   (a) ……………………………………………………………………… (1 mark)
   (b) ……………………………………………………………………… (1 mark)

14. Which were the operation days?
   ………………………………………………………………………… (1 mark)

15. How did the patients look when they came back from the operating theatre?

.... (1 mark)

16 What was the sluice room?

.... (1 mark)

17. How often were the beds made?

.... (1 mark)

18. What made the girl feel upset?

.... (1 mark)

Situation 12: Induction course

This situation is a talk given by a Personnel Officer at Baker's Biscuits, a factory that employs a large number of different types of worker. A Personnel Officer is generally in charge of interviewing people for employment, welfare and training staff.

The speaker is talking to a small group of new employees on their first day at work. The talk is part of an 'Induction Course'. Most large companies have induction courses for their new staff. Lasting a few hours or days usually, these courses give the new worker some idea of the rules and the background of the company. They help lead the new worker into the new situation, a kind of introduction to the work.

You will hear the talk twice. You should make notes as you listen. These notes will not be marked. Study the questions before listening to the talk.

In particular, read questions 14 and 15 so that you do not give the answer to 15 when you are answering the former. Notice that you need to give three examples for question 4. Although a few questions can be answered in one word, most need half-a-dozen or so to get the full answer: there are no half-marks.

INDUCTION COURSE

You will hear a talk given by a Personnel Officer at Baker's Biscuits. The speaker is talking to a small group of new employees on their first day at work. You will hear the talk twice. You should make notes as you listen. These notes will not be marked. You may write your answers at any time. At the end of the second reading you will have four minutes to complete your answers.

1. How many people are there on the Induction course?

.... (1 mark)

2. What is the Personnel Officer's name?

.... (1 mark)

3. Where in the factory are the biscuits made?

.... (1 mark)

4. Name *three* types of worker, not on the factory floor, employed by Baker's Biscuits.
   (a) .... (1 mark)
   (b) .... (1 mark)
   (c) .... (1 mark)

5. How many shifts are worked in the factory?
   .... (1 mark)

6. Give the times of the day shift.
   .... (1 mark)

7. Why are the full-time shifts so long?
   .... (1 mark)

8. Why, according to the Personnel Officer, are most of the evening-shift workers women?
   .... (1 mark)

9. Where are the workers' clock-cards kept?
   .... (1 mark)

10. How much pay is stopped if workers are more than five minutes late?
    .... (1 mark)

11. How many overalls is each worker given?
    .... (1 mark)

12. Why must the workers' hair be covered?
    .... (1 mark)

13. What must workers do, before they start work, if they have a cut on their hands?
    .... (1 mark)

14. Why are the plasters bright blue?
    .... (1 mark)

15. Apart from being blue, what else is special about the plasters?
    .... (1 mark)

16. What must a worker do if he or she sees signs of mice in the factory?
    .... (1 mark)

17. What happens to the underweight packets of biscuits?
    .... (1 mark)

18. What day is payday?
    .... (1 mark)

Situation 13: Application forms

You will hear a talk given by a Careers' Advisor on how to fill in application forms. The talk is to a group of school leavers and college leavers at a careers' session.

    You will hear the talk twice. You should make notes as you listen. These notes will not be marked.

    Study the questions before listening to the talk. Some of the questions are fairly long, so you will need to know that you are listening for the right answers.

    Notice that questions 10 and 14 require two answers. Question 4 requires you to give two reasons (there are three possible reasons). Either of the two answers will do for question 8. Question 13 asks you for three examples, from a choice of four. Finally, look carefully at question 15: the wording of the question is different from the wording of the passage.

APPLICATION FORMS

You will hear a talk given by a Careers' Advisor on how to fill in application forms. You will hear the talk twice. You should make notes as you listen. These notes will not be marked. You may write your answers at any time. At the end of the second reading you will have five minutes to complete your answers.

1. Who is Barnsfield Council holding the careers' session for?
   .... (1 mark)

2. What is the Careers' Advisor's name?
   .... (1 mark)

3. How many employers does the Careers' Advisor meet every year?
   .... (1 mark)

4. Give *two* reasons why an employer might throw away an application form.
   (a) .... (1 mark)
   (b) .... (1 mark)

5. What is the first thing to do when you get an application form?
   .... (1 mark)

6. Why should you write your answers on a separate piece of paper first?
   .... (1 mark)

7. What should you put in the section on schools?
   .... (1 mark)

8. What does putting down that you have done a paper round or a Saturday job show?
   .... (1 mark)

9. What does putting down that you have done a one-day job show?
    .... (1 mark)

10. Why do employers look at the hobbies and interests section?
    (a) .... (1 mark)
    (b) .... (1 mark)

11. What does helping run a youth club or a scout or a guide troop show?
    .... (1 mark)

12. In the section which asks for anything else you wish to say, or asks
    you why you want the job, what must you make the employer
    believe?
    .... (1 mark)

13. What are *three* other things the Careers' Advisor said you need to put
    in this section?
    (a) .... (1 mark)
    (b) .... (1 mark)
    (c) .... (1 mark)

14. Apart from teachers, who else would be useful to give you a
    reference?
    (a) .... (1 mark)
    (b) .... (1 mark)

15. What must you remember to ask those people you have chosen?
    .... (1 mark)

Situation 14: Making a telephone call

You will hear a talk given by someone who trains telephone operators and
people who work on switchboards for the Council. You will hear the talk
twice. You should make notes as you listen. These notes will not be
marked.

Study the questions before listening to the talk, so you know what to
listen for.

Note that there are *three* answers required for question 9. You need *two*
answers for questions 11 and 15, but you should not have any difficulty
because there are several to choose from. Question 14 could be tricky,
because the answer is not in the passage: it asks you to think how you
should give the numbers. Follow the examples the speaker gives.

MAKING A TELEPHONE CALL
*You will hear a talk given by someone who trains telephone operators and
people who work on switchboards for the Council. You will hear the talk twice.
You should make notes as you listen. These notes will not be marked. You may
write your answers at any time. At the end of the second reading you will have
five minutes to complete your answers.*

1. What is the speaker's name?
   .... (1 mark)

2. How can you remind yourself of what you need to say when making a telephone call?
   .... (1 mark)

3. How can you avoid sounding rude?
   .... (1 mark)

4. What should you do if they ask a question?
   .... (1 mark)

5. What should you do if they give you instructions?
   .... (1 mark)

6. What should you do if you don't understand something?
   .... (1 mark)

7. Why are the greeting at the beginning of a call and the thanks at the end of it important?
   .... (1 mark)

8. What sort of tone should you use on the telephone?
   .... (1 mark)

9. How can you stop your words running into one another?
   (a) .... (1 mark)
   (b) .... (1 mark)
   (c) .... (1 mark)

10. What should you do when giving your name over the telephone?
    .... (1 mark)

11. Give two examples of pairs of letters which sound alike.
    (a) .... (1 mark)
    (b) .... (1 mark)

12. How do you make it clear that it is the letter **S** you are saying?
    .... (1 mark)

13. If you have to give a number **5** over the telephone, how do you make it clear and avoid its being confused with **9**?
    .... (1 mark)

14. Show how you would say the following:
    (a) Fifteen .... (1 mark)
    (b) Seventy .... (1 mark)

15. What does the speaker say a good telephone manner means?
    (a) .... (1 mark)
    (b) .... (1 mark)

Situation 15: Safety at work

This is a fairly difficult passage, particularly at the start. You should follow the advice that has been given on earlier passages and use your time to study the questions. There are no 'trick questions' but many of them require several words to answer them fully. Remember, there are no half-marks, so if an answer is not full enough it is awarded nought.

SAFETY AT WORK

You will hear a talk given by a Company Safety Officer to a group of new employees. The speaker is outlining some of the basic safety rules. You will hear the talk twice. You should make notes as you listen. These notes will not be marked. You may write your answers at any time. At the end of the second reading you will have five minutes to complete your answers.

1. What must you read before starting work at the Company?
   .... (1 mark)

2. How often does the Works Safety Committee meet?
   .... (1 mark)

3. As an employee, you have certain responsibilities for safety. What are they?
   (a) .... (1 mark)
   (b) .... (1 mark)
   (c) .... (1 mark)

4. Who make regular inspections to check that no one is breaking the rules?
   (a) .... (1 mark)
   (b) .... (1 mark)

5. What does 'good housekeeping' mean in its technical sense?
   .... (1 mark)

6. Apart from special bins for general litter and combustible materials, what other bins are there?
   (a) .... (1 mark)
   (b) .... (1 mark)

7. Give *one* example mentioned of combustible material.
   .... (1 mark)

8. Name one of the materials which is recycled.
   .... (1 mark)

9. Why must you tidy up as you go along?
   .... (1 mark)

10. What should you do about any spillage?
    .... (1 mark)

11. What should be used to hold the door open if you are carrying something through?
   .... (1 mark)

12. What injury did the careless employee (the 'idiot') cause to himself?
   .... (1 mark)

13. He tried to sue the firm for negligence. Why did he lose?
   (a) .... (1 mark)
   (b) .... (1 mark)

14. You should not use your back for lifting. What should be used?
   (a) .... (1 mark)
   (b) .... (1 mark)

15. What should you do if you cannot carry a load easily?
   (a) .... (1 mark)
   (b) .... (1 mark)

16. What might people trip over, according to the speaker?
   (a) .... (1 mark)
   (b) .... (1 mark)

17. What proportion of injuries are caused by tripping and slipping?
   .... (1 mark)

18. Why was joining two wires with ordinary sellotape dangerous?
   .... (1 mark)

19. What excuse was given for using a hair-grip instead of a fuse?
   .... (1 mark)

20. Why were the electricians furious?
   .... (1 mark)

21. What should you do about defective equipment?
   (a) .... (1 mark)
   (b) .... (1 mark)

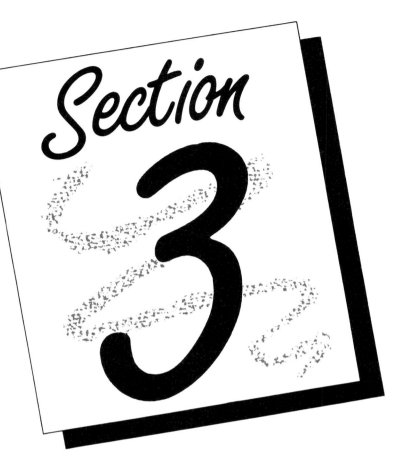

Section

3

Dictation

Dictation is where you take down the *actual words* that someone speaks to you. It is different from **summary**, where all you have to write down is the basic idea, or **selection of key information**, where you pick out the key facts and write them down in note form.

In **dictation**, however, you have to take down the complete message. Sometimes this is vital. It might be that to summarise or just select key information makes nonsense of the message.

Perhaps the message has a legal force, as in this example:

Safety in Workshops

Regulation protective goggles must be worn at all times when using any of the following equipment:

      Abrasive grinding wheels
      Cutting equipment
      Sanding discs
      Welding equipment.

Anyone failing to do so will be disciplined and may be dismissed.

Signed: G.R.E. Haverson
Works Manager

If you miss out a word such as 'regulation', people might wear swimming goggles! If you summarise 'equipment', they might not realise that 'sanding discs' are dangerous sometimes. It is difficult to see a single word in this message that is not important for some reason or another.

So taking down a message from dictation is another important skill to master. It is more difficult than the other two skills because it has to be more precise: spelling and punctuation have to be correct. Normally a message would be read at least twice, and one of the readings would be slow enough for you to get every word down. *You do not have to remember the whole thing and then write it down.*

In all the examples used in this book, the dictation passages are designed to be read three times. The first time is to get the general sense of the message. The second is a slow reading to get all the words down (with pauses, so the teacher waits a reasonable length of time until the average writer will have got words down). The third reading is for you to check on any words you have missed out or misheard.

General hints on dictation

- Don't start writing on the first reading (if the passage is to be read three times). Sit back and listen. Get the sense of what the message is about.
- Listen carefully to the voice. It will tell you not only the words but also give clues to the punctuation.
- If you miss a word, don't panic. Leave a space and put it in on the third reading.
- Write on every other line (leave a space of one line between your writing). This will make corrections easier.
- Don't worry too much about the punctuation as you are getting the message down. You can check and correct that later.
- Don't put a comma or a full stop every time the reader pauses. Check on the sense of the passage afterwards. And don't use dashes instead!

Similar words

A lot of words in English sound the same, or can sound very similar when spoken quickly. The most commonly confused words are these:

here	hear	
there	their	they're
where	wear	we're
whether	weather	
its	it's	
are	our	hour
as	has	
piece	peace	
would	wood	
to	two	too

HERE and THERE and WHERE are all concerned with a place. They can be grouped together and should be easy to remember.

'I am over **here**.' | but | 'He *hears* with his *ears*.'

'You are over **there**.' | but | 'They wear *their* overalls to work.'
They're is the same as *they are*. The apostrophe is replacing the *a*.
'They're wearing overalls' = '*They are* wearing overalls.'

'**Where** are you now?'   but   'They *wear* overalls.'
                                                  We're is the same as *we are*.
                                                  The apostrophe is replacing the
                                                  a.
                                                  'We're over here' =
                                                  '*We are* over here.'

WHETHER might remember as suggesting a question, like *why* or *who*.

'He asked **whether** I was   but   'The *weather* was awful. It rained
going out'   all day.'

ITS is the correct form to show something belonged to something else. It
is the singular form, that is *only one*, of 'their'.

'The kittens are playing with their   but   'It's very poor weather for the
ball of wool, whilst the dog   time of the year.'
jealously guards **its** bone.'   It's is the same as *it is*.
                                                  The apostrophe is replacing the
                                                  i.
                                                  '*It's raining again*' =
                                                  '*It is* raining again.'

ARE is the plural form, that is *more than one*, of 'is'.

'The kittens **are** playing.'   but   'It's not *our* dog. We haven't got
                                                  a dog. It belongs to next door.'
                                                  Hour is sixty minutes.
                                                  'When is our bus due?'
                                                  'On the *hour*.'

AS means *since*. HAS is the singular of *have*.

'We're going into town,   but   'She *has* an old pair of jeans for
as Janice has to buy some jeans.'   work but they have really had it
                                                  now for casual wear.'

PIECE can be remembered if you remember the *i* in '*bit*'.
'Peace' is the opposite of war or argument.

'Can I have another **piece** of pie,   but   'We all want world *peace*.'
please.'

WOULD is spelt in a similar way to 'should'. But in a hurry, it is easy to
write it down like 'wood', the stuff we get from trees!

'I **would** find it quite   but   'A walk through the *wood*
easy to make that mistake'   should be very pleasant.'

TO and TOO and TWO always cause problems. *Two* is the number **2** (remember the word '*twin*').

'I have **two** sisters. They are twins.'
Too is used with *too many, too much* (it has an extra '**o**').
'He took the corner **too** fast and crashed into a tree.'
To is used with direction (*to go*, *walk into*) or *to do* something.
'I want **to** go **to** the disco. I have **to** catch the bus **to** town.'

Punctuation marks: hints to remember

Full stops You use full stops at the end of a **sentence.** This is a group of words that makes complete sense.

Walking down the road. ✗ (not complete sense — *who* was walking?)

Write something like:
Two men were walking down the road. ✓

I went into town by bus it was very slow. ✗ (two complete ideas here — two full stops are needed here.)

Write:
I went into town by bus.
It was very slow. ✓

In **dictation**, you can often tell the end of a sentence by the way in which the voice falls at the end of the sentence. Then there is a pause. Then the voice starts again higher and firmer. In **letter writing**, try to keep all your sentences very short.

You use full stops with **abbreviations**, like *e.g.*, *i.e.*, *etc.*, and people's initials, *H. E. Hanson.*

But many people don't use full stops like this nowadays, particularly in fully blocked letters or with letters after someone's name.
Mr T W Wilson, MA, MSc, LLB, FRSA, AMBIM looks neater than
Mr. T. W. Wilson, M.A., M.Sc., Ll.B., F.R.S.A., A.M.B.I.M. We do not use full stops with initials in common use nowadays, like *BBC*, *ITV*, *plc* (public limited company) and *RGN* (registered general nurse). We do not use full stops with *Mr*, *Mrs*, *Miss*, *Ms* or *Dr* in front of someone's name.

Our advice is, when in doubt, leave them out.

Capital letters You have to have a capital letter to start a sentence. You need them with 99% of all abbreviations.

They should be clearly written. It is no use saying, 'But that's how I write my capitals' if someone points out they are not clear. That kind of argument is rather like saying, 'But that's the side of the road I want to drive on', if you're caught driving on the right-hand side of the road! You are still breaking the law.

So if your capitals are not clear, it is up to you to make them legible. You can't use capital letters in the middle of a word, so someone writing like this:

But That is how I write
my letters. I always
write like That ITS not
FuNNY aT all.

is wrong.

Ask the advice of your teacher about the clarity of your capitals if you have ever had any cause to think they might cause confusion. In this area of writing, you do *not* get the benefit of doubt.

Take care in particular with capital 'C' and capital 'S' — are they large enough? Other problem letters like this are 'K', 'M', 'O', 'V', 'W'. Make sure that those letters with 'tails' (these are called 'descenders'), like 'f', 'g', 'j', 'p', 'q', and 'y' have the descender *below* the line for *small* letters, and *above* the line for capitals, e.g.

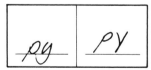

Remember that *capital means 'head'* (like capital city). A capital letter in the *middle* of a word is *always wrong*.

Questions marks If there is a direct question, that seems to expect an answer, you use a question mark at the end. It could be one word, like 'Why?', or several, like 'Is anyone going to go to that disco on Friday?' Inverted commas are almost always used as well, to show that someone's actual words are being used. (But you might find that in advertisements and newspaper articles, the inverted commas are left out.)

You do not need a question mark in a sentence with the words *wonder(ed)* or *doubt(ed)* in it:

I wonder if Cheryl will be there tonight.

I doubt whether she will manage to get there.

These are indirect questions like 'Tracey asked the shop-keeper how much longer she would be kept waiting'. In other words, they are ordinary sentences.

In dictation, you can often tell a direct question by the way in which the voice rises at the end and seems to hang there in mid-air. (In the indirect question, the voice falls, as with an ordinary sentence, so you put a full stop.)

verted commas Inverted commas, or quotation marks, are placed around someone's actual words. *John shouted, 'It wasn't me, I wasn't even there!'* In **dictation** you can often tell the actual words because they are spoken in a different tone of voice, more dramatically.

Sometimes people use inverted commas to show a false description of something or someone, as if they are being sarcastic, like

> *The pair of jeans that had been such a 'bargain' fell to pieces the first time they were washed.*

Obviously, they were not a bargain at all. Similarly,

> *Her so-called 'friend' went off and left her.*

You can hear this use easily in dictation because the reader emphasises the word in a heavy, sarcastic way.

Lastly, inverted commas are sometimes used in handwriting to indicate the title of a book, play, TV programme, etc. Whilst in print, the printer would be able to use italics (sloping print), that is not so easy in handwriting.

In print: Gran used to watch *Coronation Street* twice a week, every week.

In handwriting:

> Gran used to watch 'Coronation Street twice a week, every week.

Colon The main use of the colon is to introduce lists, though nowadays even that use is becoming less popular.

The colon (:) and the semi-colon (;) can be used to join sentences but their use is rare.

In **dictation** you can hardly ever tell whether a colon or semi-colon has been used. It is really a matter of personal style. A full stop will always be correct.

The Dash The dash (—) is used to bring in a sudden surprise idea, usually at the end of a sentence. *He was tall, dark and handsome — and he knew it.*

You can tell that it has been used in **dictation** by the sudden dramatic pause — and then the rush of words that follows it.

Brackets   Brackets (properly known as parentheses) usually introduce an afterthought or an explanation. A good reader will indicate this in **dictation** by a sort of hushed voice, as if giving a personal message, an aside. *Our next door neighbour (the one with the seven cats) died suddenly last week.* You must not forget to close the brackets off. Often you will find that a pair of commas will do instead. *Mr Simpson, our history teacher, is only 24, though he looks much older.*

Commas   Commas are used to separate items in a list, used with a colon. *She had so many things to do: shopping, feeding the cats, going to the Post Office, cleaning the windows. She did not know where to start.*

You do not need to use a comma in front of *and* with items in a list. The commas are really taking the place of *and*, like this example: *She bought the following items: eggs, butter, fish, bread and milk.*

Commas are also used to separate words or groups of words out from the rest of the sentence to make the meaning clear.

Well, Sara, fancy seeing you here.

The man, who was wearing a cap and an overcoat, disappeared silently into the crowd.

Liz felt depressed, though she did not know why.

In the above sentences, the key words are *Fancy seeing you here, The man disappeared silently into the crowd* and *Liz felt depressed.* The commas help to make that clearer.

In **dictation**, commas are shown by a slight pause, though you will have to read through and see if you have put any that do not make sense. For example, you *can't* put commas here:

Bill, was late, for work. That would split the idea up so that none of it made sense.

The apostrophe   The apostrophe (') shows that letters are missing.

It's	means	*it is*
don't	means	*do not*
wasn't	means	*was not.*

You have to be careful to put the apostrophe in the right place to show which letter is missing. Note the exception: *won't* means *will not* (several letters are missing here and mixed up, too). There are some further examples under the section on **Similar words** on page 27.

The apostrophe also shows that something *belongs* to someone or something. *Joanne's book* means the book *belongs* to Joanne, the owner. Where the apostrophe is put depends on whether the owner is *singular* (one only) or *plural* (more than one).

For *singular*, add **'s.**

The man's child (one man) or The man's children (still one man).

For *plural*, add only **'** if the word ends in **s** already.

The boys' project (several boys).

If the plural does not end in **s**, treat it like a singular. Add **'s**.
  The children's playground.
You can't tell this by listening to a dictation, only by knowing the rule.

Hyphens   The hyphen (-) is a small dash used to link two or more words together to make a new idea, like *value-for-money, do-it-yourself, red-hot.*

Dictation passages

Your teacher will read out full instructions to you. All the dictation passages cover different points of spelling discussed already.
The passages are on the following topics:

Passage 1:   Announcement   —Sales advert
Passage 2:   Announcement   —Break-in
Passage 3:   Notice   —Christmas socials
Passage 4:   Announcement   —Plants for sale
Passage 5:   Announcement   —Lost handbag
Passage 6:   Notice   —Fire exits
Passage 7:   Letter   —Safety committee
Passage 8:   Notice   —Telephone calls.

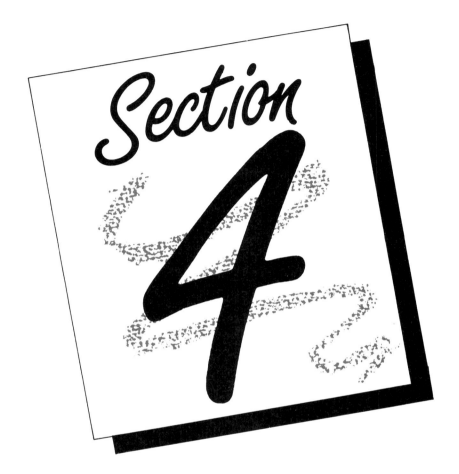

Section

4

Reading and understanding

This section also deals with understanding and summarising skills; this time reading, not listening. You will be given reading passages in the form of an advertisement, a letter or a notice for example. Not all the information is needed, and some of the questions are not straightforward.

In particular:

1. Read every word. The word *NOT* is easy to overlook.
2. Look for the same thing being said in two different ways.
3. Try to spot questions which ask for two answers.

The passages do not need to be answered in sentences. Sometimes one or two words will do. However, many of the answers will need several words to explain them.

To help you in the first two situations in this section, those questions needing more than two or three words have been marked with an asterisk (*).

General hints on reading information

- *Always read the passage through twice before looking at the questions.* It is amazing what people can miss on the first reading.

- *Always read ALL the questions through twice before answering any of them.* That stops you putting the answer for one question as the answer for another or repeating yourself. Answers to each question are usually different.

- *Read the passage a third time to remind you of what you have read already.* Keep looking back at the passage for every question.

- *Take special care with names, figures, times and dates.* They must be copied correctly. Work out any additions or subtractions on a piece of paper if necessary.

- *Leave a space if you can't decide the answer to a question at first.* Go back to it when you have finished the others.

- *Check over your work at the end.* Make sure you have not copied any words wrongly from the passage into your answers. It is easily done if you are rushing but it does spoil the work.

Situation 16: Staff lockers

*Read the following notice and then answer the questions on it that follow. Questions marked * require more than two or three words for the answers.*

*Example: *Question 5:* What will the company not take responsibility for?
Answer: any loss or damage.*

NOTICE
Staff Lockers

Lockers are provided by the company for the use of staff in connexion with their work, particularly for storing a change of clothing and other personal possessions.

Staff are reminded to keep lockers securely fastened with a small padlock and key. There have been a few instances of pilfering from lockers over the past few months, and the management can take no responsibility for any loss or damage caused.

If anyone is seen tampering with someone else's locker, he or she must be reported to the Security Department immediately. It is against company rules to interfere with someone else's locker and offenders will be dismissed.

If a locker is damaged or cannot be locked, report the matter to your supervisor as soon as possible.

Food must not be left in lockers overnight because of the danger of attracting vermin.

Staff are advised not to leave valuables in lockers at any time.

Questions

1. Who owns the lockers? .... (1 mark)
*2. What are lockers for? .... (1 mark)
*3. How should lockers be secured? .... (1 mark)
4. Why should lockers be secured? .... (1 mark)
*5. What will the company not take responsibility for? .... (1 mark)
*6. What should you do if you see someone interfering with someone else's locker? .... (1 mark)
7. What happens to someone who interferes with someone else's locker? .... (1 mark)
8. What should you do if the locker cannot be locked? .... (1 mark)
9. What must you not leave in lockers overnight and why?
   (a) What? .... (1 mark)
   (b) Why? .... (1 mark)
10. What should you never leave in lockers? .... (1 mark)

Situation 17: Printing adverts

The firm you work for wants to have some brochures printed to advertise a sale. Study the advertisements below, taken from the newspaper, and then answer the questions that follow.

HIGH·SPEED
while·you·wait
INSTA-PRINT LTD

1 copy — or 2000!

272 Dean Hill
BARNSFIELD,
BN15 2AR

Tel 9072 1463
PRINTING & COPYING

CAXTON CRAFT
GRAPHICS LIMITED

Unit 9, Central Trading Estate,
Birchill Road, Barnsfield,
W. Yorks. BN13 1HR

Quality Colour Printing & Design

0812 33555

for the complete printing service
Satisfaction Guaranteed

PHOTOFINISH LTD
WHILE-U-WAIT
INSTANT
PHOTOCOPYING
ANY SIZE
ANY QUANTITY

Bridge Street, Barnsfield, BN3 1TR

TEL 0812-91355

MAGIC PRINT LTD

★ PRINTING
★ COPYING
★ DUPLICATING
★ TYPESETTING
★ ARTWORK
★ DESIGN SERVICE
★ PLAN PRINTING
★ BINDING

21 Hill Gate,
Pressbridge
Derbyshire
PS9 8TR
Pressbridge (013-928)
For all enquiries and free quotations

bartons Printers

Specialists in
COMPUTER PRINTING

● Small quantities accepted

● For all your office requirements

Bartons Ltd.
Whitehill Industrial Estate
(off Gravesend Road)
Barnsfield BN3 2PR

Tel 0812-94266

Questions

1. Which firm is not a local firm with a Barnsfield address?...... (1 mark)
2. Which two firms in Barnsfield do copying? .... (1 mark)
*3. Which firms are on industrial estates?........................... (1 mark)
*4. Which firms give the county in their addresses?................ (1 mark)
5. Who would you contact from this list if you wanted
   (a) colour printing?.. (1 mark)
   (b) computer stationery printed? .... (1 mark)
6. Which firms will design for work for you?
   (a) .... (1 mark)
   (b) .... (1 mark)
7. If your firm was at Toll Lane, Barnsfield B15 7QX, which of these advertisers is likely to be nearest to you?
   .... (1 mark)
8. Which firm does the narrowest range of work?
   .... (1 mark)

Situation 18: New pay day

Read the following office letter (memorandum) and then answer the questions that follow.

MEMORANDUM

TO: All staff   DATE: 12 November

FROM: Manager, Accounts Dept.   REF: CA/CRP

SUBJECT: <u>New days and dates for payment of wages & salaries</u>

As you may know, a new ICM computer has been installed recently. Considerable savings in costs will be made if wages payments are 'staggered': that is, some paid one day, some the following day and so on, instead of all of them on Friday, as at present.

The changes have been agreed with staff representatives on the Joint Consultative Committee, to take effect from 1 January.

The changeover date has been chosen because it avoids disrupting staff just before Christmas and, with the holiday period, less overtime is done, so fewer calculations have to be made.

These will be the dates on which employees will now be paid:

    Maintenance and transport staff: Tuesdays
    Clerical and office staff: Wednesdays
    Canteen and welfare staff: Thursdays
    Cleaning staff: Fridays.

There will be no difference to basic weekly rates. The new system simply means that instead of working a week in hand and being paid a week later for the work done up to the previous Saturday, some staff will be paid as quickly as two working days in hand (excluding Sunday as a working day). It is possible that some overtime payments may not have been fully calculated in the first week. These *will* be paid by the following week, and after 8 January there should be no delays.

Changes will also be made to the payments of salaries to monthly staff. The majority of such staff will now be paid on the 18th of the month instead of on the 28th, 29th, 30th or 31st as at present. In effect this will be 10 to 13 days earlier. Sales representatives will, however, continue to be paid on the last day of the month.

T G Tomkins
Accounts Manager

Questions

1. What is the memorandum about? .... (2 marks for full answer)
2. What new equipment will be used in calculating wages and salaries?
   .... (1 mark)
3. Who have agreed to the changes? .... (1 mark)
4. When will the changes start? .... (1 mark)
5. Payment of wages will be 'staggered'. What does this mean? (1 mark)
6. Why has this changeover date been chosen?
   (a) .... (1 mark)
   (b) .... (1 mark)
7. Which staff will not have their wages paid on a different day? (1 mark)
8. When will Welfare staff be paid? .... (1 mark)
9. What does being paid 'a week in hand' mean? .... (1 mark)
10. Which staff will now be paid as quickly as three days in hand
    (excluding Sundays)? .... (1 mark)
11. What difficulty could occur with overtime payments in the first week?
    .... (1 mark)
12. Which staff will now be paid 10 to 13 days earlier? .... (1 mark)
13. Which staff will still be paid at the end of the month? .... (1 mark)

Situation 19: Insurance

Read the following and then answer the questions that follow.

Gary Heywood has been getting quotations for insuring his motor-cycle. It is a Honda Sports 125L.

A quotation is a calculation of how much you will pay for a year's insurance. They often vary from one company to another, depending on what kind of insurance cover you want.

For example, one kind of cover is Third Party, Fire and Theft. Gary would be insured for any injuries he caused to others, and for the bike being stolen or catching fire. Another is Comprehensive insurance: he would be insured for damage to the bike and himself as well, possibly even for the loss of tools and equipment. His age and experience will affect the amount he pays (the premium). So will any convictions or accidents, and even where he lives.

One of the quotations on page 42 is from an insurance broker — a firm specialising in advising about insurance.

AUSTEN AND ALLEN (Insurance Brokers) LTD
131 Norris Road   13 High Street
BARNSFIELD   and at BRAUNTON
BN3 2SR   BR6 1QY
Telephone: 0951-2364   Telephone: 623-1133

Mr Gary Heywood

Please reply to:
Barnsfield

We have pleasure in quoting for:

Honda   125 L (Sports)

Fully comprehensive ☑
Third Party F & T ☐

ANNUAL PREMIUM (single payment): *£ 75.00*

PREMIUMS CAN BE PAID IN UP TO SEVEN
PAYMENTS, IF REQUIRED,
E.G. DEPOSIT .... *£25* ...   THEN .... *7* ....
PAYMENTS OF .... *£15* .....
(total ... *£ 85* .... inclusive of all charges).

Premiums can be reduced by taking voluntary restriction in
cover, e.g. £10 excess (paying the first £10 of any claim). Please
contact us for details.

Questions

1. What is an insurance quotation? .... (1 mark)
2. Why do quotations vary?
   (a) .... (b) .... (1 mark for 2 examples)
   (c) .... (d) .... (1 mark for 2 examples)
   (e) .... (f) .... (1 mark for 2 examples)
3. If Gary chose only Third Party, Fire and Theft, what would he not be
   insured for?
   (a) .... (1 mark)
   (b) .... (1 mark)
   (c) .... (1 mark)

4. What is an insurance broker? .... (1 mark)
5. Austen and Allen have two branch offices. What is the telephone number of the branch Gary is dealing with? .... (1 mark)
6. What kind of insurance is Gary being quoted for? .... (1 mark)
7. What make of bike does Gary have?............................. (1 mark)
8. How much is the quotation for? .... (1 mark)
9. How much more does it cost to pay the premium by instalments?
.... (1 mark)
10. How can he reduce the premium?................................ (1 mark)
11. What is an 'excess'?.. (1 mark)

Situation 20: Court fine

Read the following and then answer the questions that follow.

Sharon Butler owns a small motorcycle. Her best friend's boyfriend often helps her with the small repairs that are needed. In return she occasionally lends him the motorcycle.

It never occurred to Sharon that the lad did not have a licence or insurance until the day he was stopped by the police. It is the owner's responsibility to check that anyone using her motorcycle is covered by insurance and has a licence.

Sharon was prosecuted by the police and received exactly the same amount of fines as the culprit himself. After the court case, Sharon was sent a notice from the court (see page 44).

PTO

METROPOLITAN DISTRICT OF BARNSFIELD

To:

Sharon Butler
Flat 2
63 Ash Tree Road
Bay Green
Barnsfield BN5 8ND

Reference No.: 2176/2186/

Date of conviction: 3 Feb. 1986

Driving Licence No: BUTLE/76 1111

Offence		Fine		Costs		Time allowed for payment
No. 1	Permit no insurance	50	00	5	00	
No. 2	Aid and abet no Driving Licence	20	00			£5.00 per week
No. 3						
No. 4						
	Total amount payable					£75.00

Driving Licence to be endorsed in respect of offence No. 1	Your licence has been forwarded to The Driver and Vehicle Licensing Centre. It will be returned to you in a few days. ✔	Offence(s) No. DISQUALIFIED from holding or obtaining a Driving Licence for a period of:

You were, on the above date, convicted of the offence(s) and ordered to pay the sum(s) set out above. Payment of the amount due should be made either by post to:

Clerk to the Justices, Barnsfield Magistrates' Court, Botham St, Barnsfield BN3 1FG, or made personally at that address during the hours of 9.30a.m. – 1.00p.m. and 2.00p.m. – 4.00p.m. Monday, Tuesday, Thursday and Friday. Closed all day Wednesday.

   THIS NOTICE MUST BE RETURNED WHEN
   FORWARDING YOUR REMITTANCE. ANY
   CORRESPONDENCE MUST QUOTE THE
   REFERENCE NUMBER AND YOUR NAME AND
   ADDRESS.

Questions

1. What reference number will Sharon have to quote if she writes to the court?.. (1 mark)
2. What is her Driving Licence number? .... (1 mark)
3. Sharon was charged with two offences. What was the first one? .... (1 mark)
4. What was the second offence? .... (1 mark)
5. How much was the total *fine*? .... (1 mark)
6. What is the weekly amount Sharon has to pay? .... (1 mark)
7. Was Sharon's Driving Licence endorsed? .... (1 mark)
8. Will she get her licence back? .... (1 mark)
9. The document suggests two ways in which payment can be made. These are:
   (a) .... (1 mark)
   (b) .... (1 mark)
10. Who should the payments be made to? .... (1 mark)
11. What time is the lunch hour at the Magistrates' Court? .... (1 mark)
12. What day is the court closed? .... (1 mark)
13. What must Sharon send with her money if she sends it by post? .... (1 mark)
14. Apart from the reference number, what else must Sharon quote if she writes to the court? .... (1 mark)

Situation 21: Coach fares

Study the following leaflet about coach fares and then answer the questions about it.

STUDENT SAVERS

To

Newcastle	**£6**
Bristol	**£10**
Plymouth	**£12**

RETURN

and many other places FROM BARNSFIELD BY EXPRESWAY COACHES Fully air-conditioned, in-travel video, etc.

DAILY Monday to Saturday

LESS THAN HALF THE RAIL FARE

Who can travel

- Students under 16 (on production of birth certificate)
- Students 16–18 in full-time education (on production of student enrolment card or letter from Headteacher*)
- Students over 18 in full-time education (on production of N.U.S. card)

How to book

Book one day in advance at Barnsfield coach station, or the local agent, Thomas's High Street.

Conditions

1. No stand-by tickets — all tickets must be booked.
2. Only one suitcase or similar per passenger†.
3. Must be full-time students.
4. Return date not guaranteed unless booked in advance.
5. Break of journey not permitted.

Single fares

Half return fare + £2

*Special forms available for certification by Headteachers.
† Excess baggage payable for at £1 per item.

Questions

1. How much would it cost for two full-time students to go to Bristol (return) if they had no excess baggage? .... (1 mark)
2. How much would it cost them for a single journey to Bristol? .... (1 mark)
3. What day(s) of the week can you not travel by Student Saver tickets? .... (1 mark)
4. What is the advantage over rail travel? .... (1 mark)
5. What age do you have to be to need to produce a birth certificate? .... (1 mark)

6. Where can you book tickets?
   (a) .... (1 mark)
   (b) .... (1 mark)
7. What happens if you have two pieces of luggage, say a suitcase and a rucksack? .... (1 mark)
8. Why should you book your return date in advance? .... (1 mark)
9. What will they not allow you to do if you are travelling on a Student Saver ticket? .... (1 mark)

Situation 22: Help lines

Read the following and then answer the questions that follow.

Many organisations offer help and advice in time of need. Often their names and addresses are available from public libraries or leaflets published by the council or Citizens' Advice Bureaux. Thompson Local Directories publish very useful lists in their telephone directories that are sent free to everyone who has a telephone. The information below is similar to the sort of information that Thompson Local Directories give. (Note: the organisations are real but the addresses and telephone numbers in this exercise have been changed and many organisations have been left out because of space.)

TELEPHONE LINES FOR ADVICE & HELP

Gamblers Anonymous: Regional Service Office, 27 Carlton Road, STRODE. Tel: 056-04456
24 hour national service for anyone who seriously wants to give up gambling.

Message Home: Tel: 056-873 9121.
This is a confidential service run by the Mothers' Union to help runaways to contact their parents. There is no need to say where you are. You just dial and give your message.

Missing Persons: Salvation Army Missing Persons Bureaux, 13 Underwood St, London EC1. Tel: 01-837 0946.
Will trace missing relatives for reconciliation purposes only. Contact London number for details of local bureau.

Samaritans: 19 High Street, STRODE. Tel: 056-66666.
A confidential service for those in despair.

PDSA (People's Dispensary for Sick Animals): Tenlock Road South, STRODE. Tel: 056-34872.

RSPCA: Waterloo Road, STRODE. Tel: 056-91277.

TELEPHONE LINES FOR FAMILY WELFARE

Age Concern: Tenby House, Princess Road, STRODE.
Tel: 056-838561.

Marriage Guidance Council: 203 Chichester Road, STRODE. Tel: 056-347891

National Council for Divorced and Separated: 17 High Street, TRENTON, Hants TR3 6PQ. *Send SAE for details of local group.*

National Council for One Parent Families: Tel: 01-881 0445 *for details & local contacts,* or write: 122 Killington Street, LONDON NC1 5FR.

NSPCC: Regional Office, 21 Waterloo Road, STRODE. Tel: 056-338891.

DISABLED

Dial UK: Telephone Advice Bureau, Strode Borough Council, Liaison Group of Volunteers, c/o Social Services Division, Town Hall, STRODE. Tel: 056: 667771 Ext. 233. *Advice service for those who are disabled and for those who care for them.*

MENCAP: The Royal Society for Mentally Handicapped Adults and Children. Regional Office: Burntwood, Lancaster Rd, Tetley, STRODE. Tel: 056-348321.

VOLUNTARY

WRVS: District Office: 4 Felton Road, STRODE. Tel: 056-235791/2 or 056-879121.

Citizens Advice Bureaux: Tetley: Passmore Road, Tetley, STRODE. Tel: 056-835431.

Strode: High Street, Strode. Tel: 056-4842091. *Offer a free and confidential service, giving advice & help on problems concerned with housing, employment, bills, and state benefits.*

Questions

1. Many organisations give help and advice if you need it. Where might you find out their addresses?
   (a) .... (b) ....
   (c) .... (d) .... (2 marks)
2. Several organisations you can contact day or night. Apart from the Samaritans, what other organisation makes it clear you can do this?
   .... (1 mark)
3. Which two organisations are situated in the same street?
   .... (1 mark)
4. How many organisations do not have an address in Strode?
   .... (1 mark)
5. Which of these organisations listed here can you not contact by telephone? .... (1 mark)
6. Which organisation will help runaways contact their parents?
   .... (1 mark)
7. Who will help trace missing persons? .... (1 mark)
8. Most organisations are completely confidential. But which organisations actually state that they offer confidentiality?
   .... (1 mark)
9. Which organisations can be contacted through the Social Services?
   .... (1 mark)
10. Which organisations are concerned with
    (a) animals .... (1 mark)
    (b) the elderly .... (1 mark)
    (c) the mentally handicapped? .... (1 mark)
11. How many telephone numbers has the WRVS in Strode? .... (1 mark)
12. Which organisation will give advice on unemployment benefits?
    .... (1 mark)

Situation 23: Bus service

Many firms, particularly in country areas, run special bus services for their workers. You are starting work with Richardsons Ltd. and they send you the letter on page 50 giving details of where to report on your first day.

Read the letter on the following page and then answer these questions to show you have understood what it says.

Questions
1. Why have you been sent this letter? .... (1 mark)
2. What is the route number of the regular bus service?......... (1 mark)
3. Where do the two buses meet? .... (1 mark)
4. How long would the journey from Braunton to the works take?
   .... (1 mark)
5. If you caught a bus to work at Higher Lane
   (a) which bus would you catch? .... (1 mark)
   (b) how long would the journey last? .... (1 mark)
6. If you had to be at work by 8 a.m., at what time would you need to catch the bus at Branklesea High Street? .... (1 mark)
7. If you finished work at 5.30 p.m., what approximate time would you expect to be at Brandlecombe Red Lion?....................... (1 mark)
8. Who should you report to on your first morning?
9. How could you find your way to C Block? .... (1 mark)
10. Which block does not have a canteen?........................... (1 mark)
11. Where are the first aid posts located? .... (1 mark)
12. Where are the Nurse and Medical Room? .... (1 mark)
13. Who should you contact if you have any questions?
    (a) .... (1 mark)
    (b) .... (1 mark)

RICHARDSONS Ltd
Brandlecombe
BRAUNTON
Lincs.
BR3 6AP   Tel: 039-8621

Date as postmark

Dear Employee

Welcome to Richardson's Ltd. I am sending you these details to help you find your way around.

Bus service
The works bus service is free and connects with the regular Eastern bus service (No. 157) from Branklesea and Braunton as shown.

No. 157	Braunton Market	*dep.*	07.00	07.30	08.00
	Branklesea High St,		07.10	07.40	08.10
	Brandlecombe Red Lion	*arr.*	07.30	08.00	08.30
Works bus	Brandlecombe Red Lion	*dep.*	07.30	08.00	08.30
	Brandlecombe Higher Lane		07.35	08.05	08.35
	Brandlecombe Cross		07.45	08.15	08.45
	Richardsons Works	*arr.*	07.55	08.25	08.55
	Depart (evening)		17.05	17.35	18.05

On arrival
On arrival on your first morning, please report to me in room 3, C Block (signposted from the bus park).

Canteens
Canteens are located in four of the five blocks: A, B, D and E. Those working in Block C will find D Block most convenient.

Medical
First-aid posts are located by the main entrance in each block, with first-aid boxes in each section. The Medical Room and Nurse are situated in A Block.

If you have any questions, please ask me or your supervisor later.

Yours sincerely

B. Cooper

B.C.Cooper
Personnel Officer

Section

5

Indexing skills

To find a book on the library shelves, or a telephone number, or a name on a long list of employees, for example, you need indexing skills. Although *not all* information is arranged in alphabetical order, *without some system* finding the right person, place or firm would be tedious, or impossible. Just compare the two lists of towns below:

List A	List B
Lincoln	*K*
Kidderminster	Kendal
Ossett	Kettering
Ledbury	Kidderminster
Nuneaton	Kirkham
Manchester	Knowsley
Morpeth	
Oldham	*L*
Kirkham	Lancaster
Lancaster	Lancing
Leatherhead	Leatherhead
Oxford	Ledbury
Kendal	Lewes
Macclesfield	Lincoln
Llandudno	Liskeard
Nottingham	Llandudno
Maidstone	
Newport	*M*
Kettering	Macclesfield
Liskeard	Maidstone
Martock	Manchester
Knowsley	Martock
Lewes	Morpeth
Lancing	
	N
	Newport
	Nottingham
	Nuneaton
	O
	Oldham
	Ossett
	Oxford

Look for *Macclesfield* in both lists. Nearly everyone spots it first in List B, then sees it in List A because it happens to be opposite. But look for Newport or Knowsley or Lancing, and the problem in List A is much greater. So we arrange much of our material in **alphabetical order**.

A   B   C   D   E   F   G   H   I   J   K   L   M

N   O   P   Q   R   S   T   U   V   W   X   Y   Z

Telephone Directory system

This is the system used in the Telephone Directory.
Firstly, all names are listed by alphabetical order of surname or firm:

    Able Cleaning Co, 46 Greek Street ....
    Baker K.M., 106 High Street...
    Charles and Tony, Hairdressers, 91 High Street ....
    Delta Furniture Ltd, London Road...
    Extra-fine Cleaners Ltd, Grasmere Road ....
    Frederick Ltd, Walkington Road ....

You can ignore three things:
    ampersands (the symbol **&** used to mean 'and')
    apostrophes (the mark **'** used to mean 'of', *Susan's father* for example)
    hyphens (the mark **-** used to link two word together, like *Do-it-yourself*)
So when you are sorting names out with any of these marks in, just treat them as if they were not there.

Situation 24: Sorting   1

Sort the following list of firms in alphabetical order:
    Baxters Ltd, Workington Street
    Henry and Hinkley Ltd, 21 High St
    Adams, P.K., 70 High St
    Trundle and Sons, 16 High St
    Cadman & Co, Solicitors, 101 High St
    Fothergill and Troughton, Estate Agents, Lansdowne Road.

Sorting 2

If several names begin with the same letter, they are then sorted by the second letter, and then the third letter, and so on.

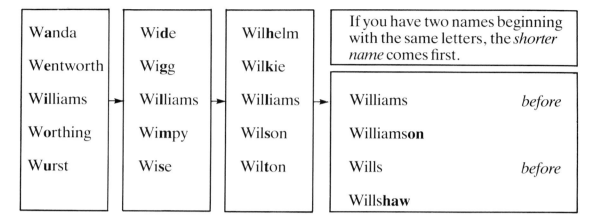

Wanda	Wide	Wilhelm	If you have two names beginning with the same letters, the *shorter name* comes first.	
Wentworth	Wigg	Wilkie		
Williams	Williams	Williams	Williams	*before*
Worthing	Wimpy	Wilson	Williamson	
Wurst	Wise	Wilton	Wills	*before*
			Willshaw	

Using the above list, put the following names in order:

Worthing Wimpey Wurst Williamson Wilton Wills
Williams Wilson Wide Wilkie Wise

Situation 25: Sorting the Macs

A rule working almost in reverse is that names beginning with Mc or Mac or M' are all treated as if spelt *Mac*.

Mable
Macarthy
McBain
McCallum
McCarthy
McCormack
McDermott
MacDiarmid
McDuff
McEwan
Macey.

Whereabouts in, before or after, that list would you put these names in their correct sequence?

McBride McInroe MacDonald's McArthur McCartney

Situation 26: Box files

Names which are made up of two words, like *Hall Green* and *Hall & Woodbridge* are listed under the first name. The second name is treated as if it was a forename, or an initial.

Genair Traffic
General Motors
Hall Green
Hall J.H.
Hall & Woodbridge
Halsons

But some names have prefixes. These are words like *St*, *de* (or *de la*), or *von* (or *van*). The rule is that all the St names go together, after Saint. All the *de* (or *De* or *De la* or *de la* names go together, i.e. all *de* will be together before any starting with Dea…) And the same applies to *van* and *von*.

Sahras ltd
Sainsbury's
Saint, K.L.
St Agnes Club
St Christopher's Vicarage
St Clair, Michael J.
St Edwards School
St George's Insurance

Day, H.J.
De Ashford, L.
de Beaufort, D.S.
de Jongh & Co
de la Cruz, A.
de la Silva
de Martini
de Silva

The following boxes represent the drawers of a card file index.

Ha to **My**	**Na** to **Peq**	**Per** to **Ry**	**Sa** to **Tam**	**Tan** to **Z**

(a) *Write the following names in their correct order under the correct heading.*

For example:

> **Tan** to **Z**
> Wessex Deliveries
> Youngs Ltd

Quigley, J.R.
Instant Service Ltd
Morris & Osbournes
Morris Q.A.

Lennox P.R.
Ryder and Jones
Jarvis and Tanzi Ltd
Wessex Deliveries

Same Day Cleaning Ltd
Sundays Ltd
Percivals Ltd
Youngs Ltd

(b) *When you have got the answers to (a), try doing the same things with this slightly more difficult example*

Sainleys & Co
van Friis, A.
van Williams
Van Hire Ltd

Jones T.W.
Saintons Ltd
Vantons

St Bernards Club
Kerry Jones Ltd
Peters & Jones Ltd

Situation 27: New customers

(a) *In the following situation, the names of five new customers have to be put in the correct order amongst the existing customers. Copy them in clearly and neatly, without misspelling any of the names or abbreviations.*

New customers: Grogans; Cutler & Sons; Underwood Bros; Sidal, A.K.; MacHenrys Ltd.

Existing customers:
   Arkwright & Sons Ltd
   Berwick Transport
   Gregsons Ltd
   Lennons (Household) Ltd
   McIntosh & Co
   Turnbull & Flack
   Vaughan, R.A.
   Yates, P.W.

(b) *A further five customers have to be added to your list. Indicate where their names should go. They are as follows:*

Vaughans Ltd; St John, B.C.; Von Arden, W.; Arnold & Taylor; McCluskie, R.

Situation 28: Telephone extensions

The following is a list of telephone extension numbers in alphabetical order. However, five staff have left, been promoted or got married. Ten new names have to be added to the list. Rewrite the list in the new correct order.

Staff who have left:
Francis; Derry; Ying; Cartwright; Adams. *Remove their names from the list.*

New staff to be added:
Underwood, Mrs A.K. Ext. 273; Davis-Hart, M., Ext. 243; Khan, S.K., Ext. 245; Masoud, Mrs D.L., Ext. 292; Harrison, P., Ext. 244; Underhill, D., Ext. 239; Masterson, Dr. M.C., Ext. 231; Young, Miss R., Ext 283; Davies, Mrs P.C., Ext. 241; Bayer, Miss R., Ext. 255.

Telephone extension numbers:

Names	Ext. numbers
Adams, Miss A.K.	273
Bell, Mrs J.W.	263
Cartwright, Miss D.L.	292
Derry, B.W.M.	283
Francis, Dr L.F.	231
Harris, Ms Y.	291
Lang, Miss R.W.	255
Masters, P.	202
Turner, Mrs R.A.	209
Walters, R.	211
Ying, S.L.	239
Yousef, Dr A.G.	272

Section

6

Form filling

A task that you will have to do many times in your life is filling in forms. There seems to be very little you can do these days without being given a form to complete. Even booking a holiday can mean you have to fill in a form.

Nearly every form you complete is a request for something, like a loan, hire purchase, a mortgage, or a job. It is therefore important that you take a great deal of care over them.

Many people do not take much care and therefore make a complete mess of the forms they are given. This is a pity. If they had just followed a *few simple rules* they would have done a better job.

The first thing to do is to read through the form before you start to fill it in. **Read the instructions.** Most of them are simple, but some can be quite hard to understand. If that is the case, then do not fill it in until you have had someone explain.

There are a number of common instructions on forms. It is important to obey them if you want the effort of filling in the form to be worthwhile.

Sometimes a form instructs you to use **block letters** or **capitals.** This often happens in the section where they want your name and address. The form asks for this because it is sometimes hard to read handwriting. Capital letters are easier to read, and the reader can then be sure that he has got all the spellings right.

Another instruction that often occurs is where you are asked to **use black ink.** The form asks for black ink rather than blue or pencil because it is going to be photocopied. Black ink copies better than blue. Pencil sometimes does not show up at all on a photocopy.

Sometimes you are instructed to **tick a box.** If that is so then you must use a tick. Even if they ask you to mark a box, you should use a tick. A cross could mean 'this is the one I want' or 'this is *not* the one I want'. A tick has no such problems. We have all been taught that it means 'correct' or 'yes'.

You can also be asked to '**delete as applicable**', or '**delete as necessary**' or '**please delete**'. 'Delete' means cross out. If you want the reader to understand exactly what you mean, you should follow the instruction. Cross out, with a single clear line, the words which do not apply to you. Do not underline them as that could mean you prefer those words. Do not put them in brackets either. Using brackets for wrong words or words which are not wanted means nothing to most people. They could even think they were the words you wanted.

If you need to **correct mistakes** in your entries on the form, cross them out clearly. This is done by putting a single line through the errors. Do not scribble them out as that looks messy. Do not underline mistakes or put them in brackets because it will not be clear that you do not wish those words to be read.

If you miss out words or letters and need to insert them, write them above the place they need to go. Then show the exact placing of the correction by using a symbol. For examples of corrected errors see below.

On many forms there are some **sections which do not apply.** If this is the case, and you are sure you do not need to fill the sections in, put a diagonal line through them.

Don't forget to sign the form, and when you put the date, write it in full. Advice on dates is given on page 71.

Situation 29: Hostel booking

A group of you, three girls and three boys, plan a weekend's youth hostelling on Friday and Saturday nights in early June. You are all between the ages of 16 and 21 (i.e. 'Juniors' as far as the Youth Hostels' Association is concerned).

You plan to go to Cheddar Youth Hostel on the evening of Friday 8 June. You hope to arrive in time for the evening meal.

None of you wish to bother with cooking or looking for somewhere to eat in the day. You therefore decide to rely entirely on Youth Hostel meals and lunch packs. This also means you don't have to worry about ordering bread or milk.

You will leave the hostel after breakfast on Sunday, but you won't get home until late afternoon so you will need to take a packed lunch.

Fill in the Hostel Booking Letter which you will be supplied with to make the reservation.

Situation 30: The electoral register

Your mother's aunt, Mrs Mavis Edna Penrose, was sixty-five on 16 July, 1985. When you visited her to wish her a happy birthday she showed you a form. It was from the Town Hall asking for details about those who live in the household so that they might be put on the Register of Electors.

No one may vote at elections to Parliament, local councils or the European Assembly unless his/her name appears on a register of electors. Your mother's aunt knows how important it is that most people take part in deciding who should be their Member of Parliament or local councillor, so she wants to fill out the form. Sadly, her eyesight is not as good as it was, so she asks you to do it for her.

Also living with your mother's aunt is her son, Michael Geoffrey Penrose who is forty-six, away on holiday at the moment, and a lodger, David Clark aged fifty. There are no other residents at her house, 69 Portland Road, Barnsfield BN7 5DG.

Fill in the form the the Register of Electors 1986 which you will be supplied with, leaving a space for your mother's aunt's signature.

Situation 31: Lost property

On Wednesday, 12 February in the city centre at Barnsfield, you boarded the 92 bus to Dene. You were going to Dene to see a friend.

The bus left at 11.15 a.m. Twenty minutes later, as the bus approached the pretty village of Holt, a fight broke out between two of the passengers.

As the fight became more violent you decided to get off the bus at the Ship Inn in Holt. You later discovered that you had left your bag on the bus. It had in it all your revision notes for your examinations.

You are very fond of that bag as it is an old canvas gas-mask container from the Second World War that your granddad had given you, and is therefore quite rare.

Later that day you went to the Lost Property Office at Barnsfield Transport Headquarters and asked if it had been handed in. The inspector you spoke to said it had not yet been handed in, but the bus driver and conductor would probably bring it in at the end of their shift.

He asked you to fill out a form giving details of the lost property and said he would contact you if the crew brought it in later.

Fill in the form which you will be supplied with using the information given above and use your own details where necessary.

Situation 32: Accident report

You work in the Production Department at Townsend, Thompson & Co. Your payroll number is 78531.

Last night, when you were leaving work, you knocked off your bike. The accident happened just inside the main gates. A visitor to the firm was leaving in his car and his front bumper just caught your rear wheel.

Last night, when you were leaving work, you were knocked off your bike. The accident happened just inside the main gates. A visitor to the firm was leaving in his car and his front bumper just caught your rear wheel.

Fortunately, you were not really injured. You grazed your left knee and your left hand slightly. Your bike was undamaged.

The Safety Officer, Mr Casey, witnessed the accident. He took you back into his office. After washing the grazes and putting a couple of plasters on them, he gave you a cup of tea. He then gave you the Minor Injury form to complete and hand in today. He told you to see your doctor if you felt any pain or discomfort. But you felt quite all right when you got home, so you did not bother.

Fill in the form which you will be supplied with giving the information above and use your own details where necessary.

Situation 33: Booking an ambulance

As part of your school or college course it has been arranged for you to take part in a work experience scheme. For two weeks you are to work in the Outpatients' Department at a local hospital. Your duties include 'booking' the patients in as they come for their appointments and doing some of the clerical tasks needed in a busy hospital.

One of your jobs is to book the ambulances needed for the patients' next visits. John David Bailey, aged 19, has a broken right leg but can manage to walk if he uses crutches. He has to come to Mr Wilson's Fracture Clinic, St John's Hospital, at 9.30 a.m. on Monday, 20 November. He lives at 14 Winnock Close, Barnsfield BN2 2NN. He is expected to need an ambulance to take him home at 12 midday.

Fill in the Ambulance Booking Form which you will be supplied with using the information given above.

Situation 34: Job application

The following advertisement appeared in the Barnsfield local paper, the *Barnsfield Advertiser.*

Packing Room Assistant

Reliable young person to work in the packing room of the Audio-Visual Discount Centre, Commercial St, Barnsfield BN3 2GD.

The shop sells records, cassettes, and video-cassettes at discount prices to the public. Packing room duties include checking and ordering stock, and packing the customers' orders. Some record-keeping for the 'Top-Ten' sales charts is also needed.

The wages are £60.00 per week for a forty-hour, five-day week. Suit school or college leaver with an interest in the record business.

Application forms from Miss Sindhu, Manager, Audio-Visual Discount Centre, at the above address.

Fill in the form which you will be supplied with using your own details and the information given above.

Situation 35: Hire purchase

As you have a weekend job as a cashier for a local garage which earns you £25.00 per week, you decide to buy yourself a new stereo system. The system you like, a Pinason 90, is now being sold at the very reasonable price of £336.00 on Hire Purchase. You could easily manage the £14.00 per month repayments for the next twenty-four months.

As you are under eighteen you cannot enter into a Hire Purchase Agreement without the help of a parent or guardian. He or she has to be willing to guarantee the payments. However, one of your parents or your guardian is willing to do this for you.

If you would rather not give personal details you can assume your name is John or Joan Smith. You are sixteen years old and were born on 15 March. Your mother, Jean Smith, was born on the same date forty years ago. She works at K. Macdonald & Son, Oldtree Lane, Barnsfield BN16 8BB. She is a supervisor earning £9,000 per year.

The garage where you work is 'Parton Petrol', Parton Road, Barnsfield.

You both live at 182 Edith Road, Barnsfield BN18 5PE, which you moved to last February. Before that you lived at 119 Grammar Street, Barnsfield BN6 7PH.

You will be supplied with an 'Application for Hire Purchase' form. Complete Part A using the details given above. Complete Part B for your parent or guardian, leaving a space for the signature.

Situation 36: Applying for a council house

Your cousin, Sophie Sands, is eighteen and married to nineteen-year-old David Sands. They have a little boy, Darren Craig, who is fifteen months old.

Sophie and David could not manage to find a home of their own when they got married. They live with David's parents at 23 Gorton Road, Ardton, Barnsfield BN6 3RS. This makes life quite hard as young Darren has to share their small bedroom. They have to wait their turn to use the kitchen and bathroom. David's parents and brother and sister say they must have first use.

David's mother has now started to complain about the mess the little boy makes. This leads to family quarrels.

A friend told David that as he has lived in Barnsfield all his life he should be able to get a council house. Applicants are allowed a choice of which council estate they would like to live on. They can say which type of house they prefer.

David and Sophie would accept any kind of home that gave them two bedrooms. They would prefer to live on the Parton estate, but would not mind living in Bay Green or even Oldcliffe. If they had no other choice they would accept a place in Ardton. Neither Sophie nor David could stand to live in Greenbank or Grimesthorne.

Sophie called in at the council's Housing Department and was given a form to complete. Unfortunately, neither David nor Sophie was very good at school work and both of them find the form very difficult. You agree to help them make the application.

On David's behalf, complete the 'Application for a Council Dwelling' form which you will be supplied with, leaving a space for his signature.

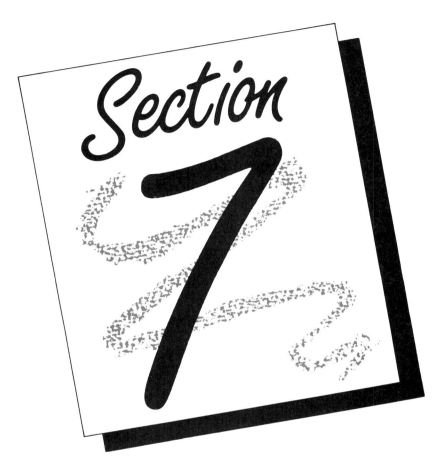

Section

7

Letter writing

It's a fact that all of us have, at some point in our lives, to write letters. The telephone is very useful, but it costs a lot for long distances. Sometimes the line seems always engaged. Sometimes the person you want is never there. Sometimes you need *legal proof* you have written. So you write a letter and get it photocopied before you send it.

You need letters, now and in later life, for all sorts of reasons.

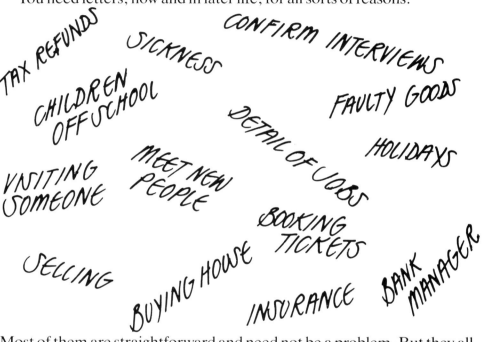

Most of them are straightforward and need not be a problem. But they all have rules, and the rules you learn now will stand you in good stead for the rest of your life. It's simply a skill, like learning to swim or ride a motorbike. Once the rules are mastered, you need never feel like an idiot again! So this section deals with the basic rules, cuts out a lot of waffle that is talked about letters, and is a 'working kit' for 99% of the letters anyone will need to write.

Letters need not be long. In fact, some of the best business letters may be only two or three lines long. But they all need three things:

Your address

Flat 2
5 Grasmere Road,
Hillington,
BARNSFIELD,
S. Yorks.
BN3 3PQ

The date

Your name and signature

It usually helps — certainly with business letters — to add *their* address too. That helps you remember who you were writing to, when you look at the copy later.

Rule 1: Your address

Never put your own name above your address (you've got it at the end!) Your address always comes *first* in a letter.

The rules for punctuation are simpler now than in your parents' day. You have a choice:

Either no punctuation at all:

191 Clarendon Street
Exley
BRIGCHESTER
Dorset
DT19 2RR

Or a comma at the end of each line:

17 Felham Walk,
TONCHESTER,
Hants,
TC9 8RY

If you like, you can make the address 'sloping':

Grassmere,
12 Twemlow Drive,
BRIGSTONE,
Leics,
BN4 4RX

But there is no need, and a straight address looks neater.

Always give as much information as you can in the address:

Flat number or House name (if any)
House number or Block name
Street, Road, Drive, Avenue, Lane name
District (if any)
MAIN POSTAL DISTRICT (town or city)
County
POST CODE in capitals

Some towns or cities do not need the county. These are places like London, Birmingham, Manchester, Edinburgh.

All addresses need a **post code**. You can find out your post code if you do not know it by telephoning the number given under the Post Office in your telephone directory.

Your address is written in the top right-hand corner of your letter, leaving a 15mm margin all the way round.

Flat 9
Carlton Towers
Westering Road
HINLEY
Cheshire
CE12 8BW
12 November 1989

There *is* another position which we'll look at later, in the **fully blocked letter.**

Rule 2: Date

Lots of different ways of writing dates have been developed over the
years. One of the most confusing forms is used in the U.S.A., where the
month is put first (October 12, 1948): If you abbreviate that, it becomes
10.12.48, which most of us would read as the tenth of December 1948. So
the first thing is never to abbreviate the date; always give it in full. The
easiest version, which is *always* acceptable, is like this: 13 March 1967.

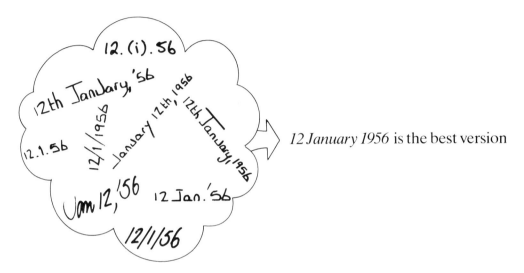

12 January 1956 is the best version

The date is always put so the *first number* is directly under the *first letter* of
your address. (Leave a space so it does not get mixed up with your post
code.)

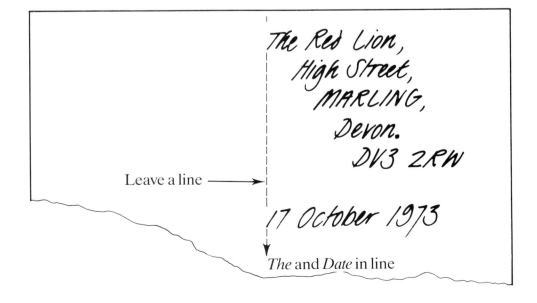

Leave a line

The and *Date* in line

Rule 3: Your name and signature

Most people practice signatures that can't be read. It is therefore only commonsense to print your name underneath. Women generally add their title, Ms, Mrs, Miss. It saves embarrassing confusion later.

It is common in formal letters and among older people just to use the initials of your forenames. Without *Ms, Mrs or Miss* in that case, most people would assume the writer to be a man. (Men do *not* write 'Mr' with their name. There is no logical reason nowadays, but it is just not thought correct. It is merely one of the *conventions* of letter writing, one of the rules that has developed over the years.)

A growing convention is for people to be less formal in letters, use modern language and sign the letter with their forename as well as with their surname. If you want to project a more modern image, this is the practice to adopt.

All the following signatures and names are quite acceptable.

Yours faithfully
J.E.Ellison
J. E. ELLISON

Yours faithfully
T. R. Timpson
MRS. T. R. TIMPSON

Yours faithfully
S. K. Kauser (Mrs)
S. K. KAUSER (MRS)

Yours faithfully,
Joanne Reed
(MISS) JOANNE REED

Yours sincerely
Tom Blyth
T. J. R. BLYTH

Yours sincerely
LS Young
L. S. YOUNG

Yours sincerely
Michael Soo
MICHAEL SOO

Yours sincerely
Suraya Mistry.
SURAYA MISTRY

Yours sincerely
Byrony Evans.
B. EVANS (MS)

Yours sincerely
Mike Collinson
T. MICHAEL COLLINSON

Rule 4: Starting and ending the letter

Starting and ending the letter used to be a problem, with all sorts of different endings like 'Yours truly' and 'Your obedient servant'.

Nowadays, life is simpler, though you will find many terms still in use. For example, the Start to the letter is sometimes called the Salutation, Greeting or Opening. The convention is that letters start with 'Dear …', even if they are unfriendly.

Sometimes you find that firms use word-processors to send out circular letters advertising their products. Sometimes this sort of letter might avoid 'Dear'. Instead, it might say something like, 'Have you ever thought, Mrs Jones, how much money you spend on heating your roof?'

However, for most purposes we still start the letter with 'Dear …'. We could use the forename, or title (Mr, Mrs, Ms or Miss) with the surname, or a formal term like 'Sir'.

Which we use depends on how formal the letter is and how well you know the person reading it. For example, you might know that a teacher's name is 'Dave' or 'Linda', but you would write to them as 'Dear Mr Baxter' or 'Dear Mrs Weiss'. But it would sound silly to write to your cousin or a friend using their surname, unless for a joke.

So use the first name only for a friendly, chatty letter. Use the surname (with Mr, Mrs, Ms or Miss) if it is anything more formal.

For very formal letters (resignation, for example), or where you do not know the reader at all, you write 'Dear Sir' ('Dear Madam' if you know it is a woman). If you do not know whether the reader if a man or a woman, the convention is to write 'Dear Sir' in your first letter. Most people adopt that practice, though some do so a little unhappily, because women hold jobs as managers, accountants, etc.

It is likely therefore that the form 'Dear Sir/Madam' becomes increasingly popular. But do avoid 'Dear Sir or Madam'—it seems to suggest you can't make up your mind.

To a firm you have a choice. You can either write 'Dear Sirs', or you can write to a specific person and say 'Dear Sir', 'Dear Madam', 'Dear Sir/ Madam' as above. It is quite common in businesses today, however, to write 'Dear Miss Halpin' or 'Dear Mr Khan' just on the strength of knowing someone from a telephone call.

Senior executives often write to each other as 'Dear Frank' or 'Dear Janet' even in formal letters. In local government (and some of the older-fashioned institutions like some solicitors or insurance companies), you might write 'Dear Sir' or 'Dear Sirs' and write above it the name of the person you are dealing with, like this:

For the attention of Mr Hammond	*The 'Dear Sirs' refers*
Dear Sirs,	*to the whole firm.*

or like this:

For the attention of Mrs Kelvin	*The 'Dear Sir' refers*
Dear Sir,	*to the head of the council department.*

So, for business letters, the following are correct.

Mrs M R Waldron,
Personnel Manager,
Timleys Ltd,
110-114 Graystone Road,
WALLINGTON,
Berks, WG3 5TF

Dear Madam,

Chief Environmental Health
Officer,
Department of Environmental
Health,
Kennington Borough Council,
Town Hall,
KENNINGTON,
Lancs, KG9 5HT

For the attention of Mrs Parveen

Dear Sir

Western United Transport Ltd,
Whitehill Industrial Estate,
TORMOUTH,
Cornwall,
TO7 7BB

Dear Sirs,

The Depot Manager,
Western United Transport Ltd,
Whitehill Industrial Estate,
TORMOUTH,
Cornwall, TO7 7BB

Dear Sir,

Dobson and Parkers (Solicitors),
4 The Arcade,
High Street,
ABERFYLLIN,
Clywd, AN17 4BV

For the attention of Ms Brewer

Dear Sirs,

The Manager,
Just a Second (Retailers) Ltd,
High Street,
BURLEY,
Cumbria,
BY13 7FG

Dear Sir/Madam,

If you know them, of course, you would write the address and start like this:

Mr J R Johnson,
Branch Manager,
Boons Superstore Ltd,
The Fairway,
SANDLEY,
Derbys., SD8 5QT

← | ALWAYS LEAVE A SPACE |

Dear Mr Johnson,

The letter Ending is even simpler. If you have used their *name*, end it with *Yours sincerely* and your signature and name. If you have used *Sir*, *Sirs*, *Sir/Madam* or *Madam*, end it with *Yours faithfully*.

These two endings — often called Complimentary Closes, or Subscriptions — always have a capital '*Y*' to start. The '*f*' of *faithfully* is always a small '*f*'. The '*s*' of *sincerely* is always a small '*s*'. Look carefully at the spelling of the two words:

  faith-ful-ly (two '*l*'s, no '*e*')
  sincere-ly   (*ere*, not *ley*)

People are always misspelling these words.

The Ending goes in the centre of your page, above your signature and name, like this:

Centrefold of page

There *is* another position for the ending, which we'll look at later in the
fully blocked letter.

Rule 5: Reader's address

If you are writing to a firm, or the Council for example, you always put the **reader's address** on your letter. Any formal or business letter has the reader's address on it. Normally you are going to keep a photocopy of it anyway, so it helps you.

It also helps the Post Office if the envelope is damaged. And it helps the firm, if the reader's name and position is on it, too. That helps them sort it quickly to the right department.

Everything we've said about *your address* (post code, etc.) is just as true here.

The reader's address always goes on the left side of the letter, usually just above the Start. Don't forget to leave a space between the address and the Start. (We gave lots of examples earlier, on page 75.)

You *may* come across some firms who put the reader's address in the bottom left-hand corner, below the Ending. But there really is no need to copy this practice: it is rather old-fashioned now, though not incorrect.

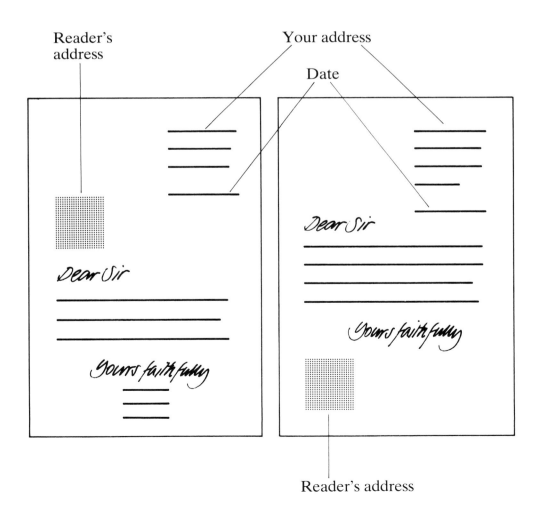

Reader's address

Your address

Date

Dear Sir

Yours faithfully

Dear Sir

Yours faithfully

Reader's address

Rule 6: Commas and margins

The rule for **commas** is very straightforward:
If *you want to use commas* at the end of each line in your *address,* you *must* use commas after

  Reader's address (every line except post code);
  the Start (after Dear Sir, etc.);
  the Ending (after Yours faithfully).

And *you have to use commas* if you use the sloping address style:

119 Charlton Street,
  Hingley,
    STRODE,
      Kent,
        SR3 6JL

If you use commas, *you have to indent your paragraphs* 15mm from your left-hand margin. That means you start your first paragraph under the 'S' of Dear Sir, or the 'M' of Dear Madam or Dear Miss Jones. It means that all your next paragraphs start 15mm in, too. A little care and trouble taken here will make a great different to the neatness of your letter.

19 Horton Road,
Barnborough,
Glos,
BA3 8PH

12 December 1987

Mrs. U. R. Wainwright,
Personnel Manager,
Briggs Marketing Ltd.,
New Purley Way,
BARNBOROUGH,
Glos,
BA8 4NR

Dear Madam,
        Thank you for your letter dated 11 December
1987, inviting me for interview on Friday 15
December.
        I shall be pleased to attend at 11.30 a.m.,
as requested.
                Yours faithfully,
                Darren Williams

                DARREN WILLIAMS

If you decide *not* to use commas, make sure you do *not* use them in the Reader's address, after the Start or after the Ending. It really isn't very logical to mix the styles.

But you can keep the paragraphs indented 15mm. In fact, this is the usual practice. The Ending remains in the centre as before.

One further version we've mentioned before is the **fully blocked style**. Many people use this because it is quite common for typewritten letters. It certainly looks quite neat, and it saves bothering with commas or margins at all.

Everything is written on the left-hand margin. You have to be a little careful with your spacing, to make sure all the details are clear. But it is an acceptable, modern style.

---

3 Blackfriars Walk
TAMBRIDGE
Herts
TA9 3RE
*

12 May 1989
*

Mr A Mehta
Branch Manager
South & Western Electrical Ltd
17 High Street
TAMBRIDGE
Herts
TA4 4GF
**

Dear Sir
*

I called into your shop on Saturday 11 May to see you, to complain about the delay in repairing my tape deck. You were, however, not available, so I told the assistant I would write.
*

The tape deck is an Elektron Mk.II, number 435813. It was supposed to be ready two weeks ago. I brought it in on 14 April.
*

Can you please hurry this repair up and tell me when I can collect it? It is very inconvenient to have to keep calling in.
**

Yours faithfully

Marie Rose

M R Rose (Mrs)

---

* At least one line's space.   **At least two lines' space.

Rule 7: References, telephone numbers and subject headings

Sometimes a firm writing you gives a **Reference** number or letters. Sometimes you are asked to quote a Reference in an advertisement. Reference is often abbreviated to 'Ref.'.

If you are given a 'Ref.', always quote it back. It saves a lot of time and bother. You *can* mention it in the body of the letter. But another place to mention it is on the left-hand margin, opposite the date in the usual letter. In the Fully Blocked Letter, you can put it above the date (leave a space). Call it 'Your ref.' and quote it in full.

If you want to give your **telephone number**, call it 'Tel.' and write it under the post code with the same spacing you would use for the date. Leave a space between the post code and the telephone number, and a space again before you write the date.

If you want to give a **subject heading** to your letter, write it below the start of the letter but before your first paragraph. Again, leave a space below and above. Subject headings are very useful, to show people what you are writing about. So the complete letter would look something like the example on the opposite page:

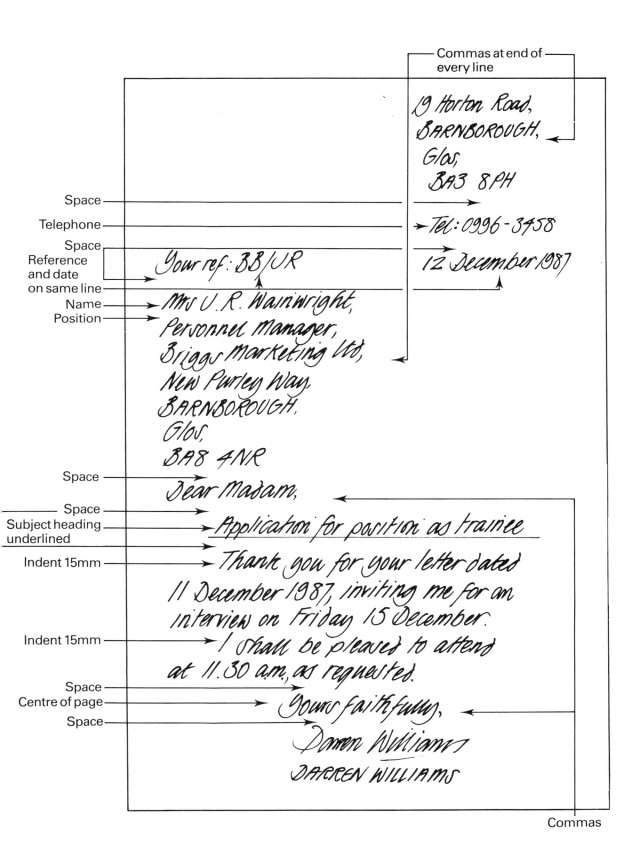

Commas at end of every line

19 Horton Road,
BARNBOROUGH,
Glos,
BA3 8PH

Space

Telephone — Tel: 0996-3458

Space
Reference and date on same line — Your ref: BB/UR   12 December 1987

Name — Mrs U.R. Wainwright,
Position — Personnel Manager,
Briggs Marketing Ltd,
New Purley Way,
BARNBOROUGH,
Glos,
BA8 4NR

Space — Dear Madam,

Space
Subject heading underlined — Application for position as trainee

Indent 15mm — Thank you for your letter dated 11 December 1987, inviting me for an interview on Friday 15 December.
Indent 15mm — I shall be pleased to attend at 11.30 a.m, as requested.

Space
Centre of page — Yours faithfully,
Space

Darren Williams
DARREN WILLIAMS

Commas

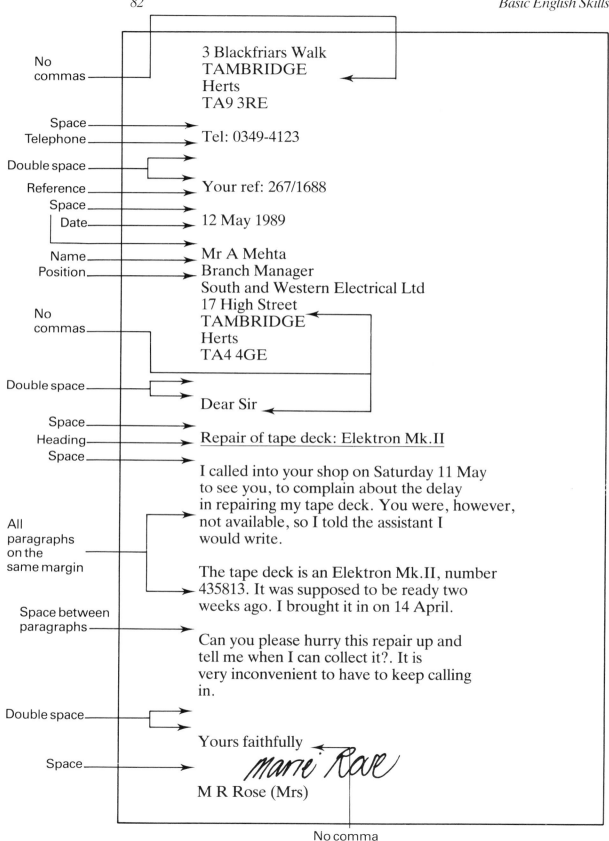

No
commas →

3 Blackfriars Walk
TAMBRIDGE
Herts
TA9 3RE

Space →
Telephone → Tel: 0349-4123

Double space →

Reference → Your ref: 267/1688
Space →
Date → 12 May 1989

Name → Mr A Mehta
Position → Branch Manager
South and Western Electrical Ltd
17 High Street
No
commas → TAMBRIDGE
Herts
TA4 4GE

Double space →

Dear Sir

Space →
Heading → Repair of tape deck: Elektron Mk.II
Space →

All
paragraphs
on the
same margin → I called into your shop on Saturday 11 May
to see you, to complain about the delay
in repairing my tape deck. You were, however,
not available, so I told the assistant I
would write.

The tape deck is an Elektron Mk.II, number
435813. It was supposed to be ready two
weeks ago. I brought it in on 14 April.

Space between
paragraphs → Can you please hurry this repair up and
tell me when I can collect it?. It is
very inconvenient to have to keep calling
in.

Double space →

Yours faithfully

Space → *Marie Rose*

M R Rose (Mrs)

No comma

Practice exercise

Below is a list of the types of errors that students commonly make. Write the correct version, to show that you understand where the mistakes are. (Sometimes there are two, sometimes there are three, mistakes in each example.)

1. *Your address*   See Rules 1 and 6.

Jayne White
Flat 3
27 Hilton Road,
ABERGURIG,
Dyfed,
AG3 9BR

✗   ✓

2. *Your address*   See Rules 2 and 7.

12 Birston Road,
Weston,
HILLINGTON,
Warwickshire,
HN8 2QZ
12/3/87
Tel: 0249-2934

✗   ✓

3. *Starting and Ending*   See Rule 4.

Dear Miss Jones,
        Thank you for your

Yours faithfully,
Mary Smith
MISS M. SMITH

✗   ✓

4. *Starting and Ending*   See Rule 4.

Dear Mr Green

Yours Sincereley

✗   ✓

5. *Reader's address*   See Rules 4 and 6.

Greyfriars Tours Ltd
Tonnington Road
DUNTON-ON-SEA,
Lincs
DS10 1BY

Dear Sir/Madam

✗   ✓

6. *Reader's address and Start*   *See Rules 4 and 6.*

Austen and Spicer (Insurance Brokers),
12 Wedgewood Way,
LONDON,
EC12 9RE
For the attention of Miss Hampton
Dear Miss Hampton

X ✓

7. *Your address and Reader's address*   *See Rules 6 and 7.*

11 Warwick Way,
TROWTON,
Somerset,
TW6 1RC

12 September 1958

Your ref: BB/KN

Mrs S. Swinton
Manager
Greenfields Ltd
High Street
TROWTON
Somerset TW1 7LW

X ✓

8. *Reader's address*   *See Rule 4.*

Mrs S. Swinton
Manager
Greenfields Ltd
High Street
TROWTON
Somerset TW1 7LW
Dear Sir/Madam

X ✓

9. *Starting and Ending*   *See Rules 4 and 6.*

Dear S. Swinton

Thank you for your forms

Yours sincerely
B. M. Kavanagh

X ✓

10. *Reader's address and Start*   *See examples given.*

Arnold's Ltd,
Tungstone Road,
GRIMLEY,
Kent,
GY9 4QA

Dear Mr Thomas,

X ✓

Situation 37: Interview

You have applied for a job as a trainee in Fenton's, a large store in town, and receive the following reply.

Fenton's Stores Ltd
Market Street
BARCHESTER
BR9 9XB

Tel: 087-6666
Ext: 2456

Date as postmark

Dear Applicant

Vacancy for Stores Trainee

Thank you for your application, which we have received with interest. We should like you to attend for interview on Thursday 10 May at 10 a.m.

If this is not convenient for any reason, would you please write and tell us, suggesting a suitable time the following week. (Please do not telephone. Please reply by first-class post.) It is helpful if you can suggest two or three times, after 10.00 a.m. and before 4.00 p.m.

If you are no longer interested in the vacancy, please inform us.

Yours sincerely

Marjorie Ashburton.

Mrs M A Ashburton
Personnel Officer

You *are* interested in the vacancy but unfortunately that day is the very day that your mother is going into hospital, and you promised you would go with her. She says it doesn't matter, she can manage — but you would rather go with her, to see everything is all right.

Write a polite letter to Mrs Ashburton, explaining the circumstances and offering alternative interview dates.

Situation 38: Record deck

You bought a record deck from Electrical Discounts Ltd, in the High Street of the town where you live. You had it for fifteen months and then the speed started to vary. So you took it back to the shop, and the Manager, Mr Black, explained that the guarantee had in fact expired but they would repair it for you at a reasonable price. It normally took two weeks, and they would send you a postcard when it was ready.

That was exactly a month ago and you have heard nothing since. You have tried ringing but the phone always seems engaged. The last time you 'phoned, last Friday, the girl who answered was very offhand and said she did not know anything about it. She said she could not find any trace of your repair order.

Because it is quite a long bus ride into this part of town you decide to *write to the Manager to ask about your repair and to mention the difficulties you have had in contacting them.* Your record deck is an Elektrikon 759, serial number 9583188.

Use your own name and address. You may assume that the shop's post code is HT7 9BS.

Situation 39: Fan club

On behalf of a group of you, *write a letter to a Fan Club you would like to join, asking for details of membership, costs and benefits.* Use your own address.

You will need to supply the details of which Fan Club you are interested in, but the address to write to is as follows:

————— Fan Club
208 Highway
Norden
LONDON SE11 1BR

The names of the people who would like to join are Debbie and Andrea Smith, yourself, Joanne Jackson, Tony Wilson, Pete Williams. Sign the letter with your name first and the others in alphabetical order beneath.

Situation 40: Youth hostel

The Wardens of Youth Hostels are very friendly but very busy people. You only use the telephone to contact them if you really have to. Imagine that you have decided to visit the Youth Hostel at Cheddar (see Situation 29, page 61).

   The details show that there is no railway station at Cheddar but there is a bus service. *Write a polite letter to the Warden (the address is given in the details that your teacher will give you), asking what the local bus service is like to the Hostel, and whether travelling back on Sunday will present any problems.* Ask what the local attractions are like — will you need special equipment for walking or visiting the caves? Don't forget you must include a stamped, addressed envelope!

Situation 41: Library book

You receive the following postcard from your local library:

Barnsfield Cultural and Recreational Services Department
Tunley Branch Library, Coulsdon Road, Tunley,
BARNSFIELD BN2 1XC

According to our records, the following book is now seriously overdue. We have written to you three times and unless you return the book and pay the amount overdue, we shall be forced to take legal action against you.

Title of book	Author	Value	Amount overdue
Roman Britain	J. W. Wentworth	£12.95	£3.75

If the book has been lost or damaged, please remit the value in full, returning this card with your remittance. Unless we hear from you within five days, the matter will be referred to the Legal Department.

This does sound very heavy-handed, particularly as you have never had this book, nor any reminders before. In fact, you have not got any books out at all at the moment, since you lost your tickets about three months ago

   You decide to send the card back, with a letter explaining the situation. *Write to the Branch Librarian, Tunley Branch Library, at the above address.*

Situation 42: Charity fund-raising

You recently heard a talk by one of the organisers of a charity organisation about the work they do. A group of you were talking about it afterwards and discussing whether you could help raise funds. The idea cropped up that you spend a fortnight, working after school/college and at weekends, doing odd jobs for people — painting, gardening, shifting rubbish, cleaning windows and cars, shopping or baby-sitting, or anything really. You would charge £1 an hour, and give all the proceeds to charity.

You can organise about ten or a dozen people to help. You can take circular letters round all the local houses near where you and your friends live, and people will only have to telephone in. Your friend Debbie can't do any heavy work because she is handicapped. She does have a telephone and can take messages and contact the others, so she is elected co-ordinator. Her mother can take messages during the day. (Their number is 09-21611.)

You call yourselves 'Oldbury Charity Action Group', after the district in which you live. When you have taken letters round, you will call round again to see people. But the important thing is to get the letter sorted out first. Using Debbie's address (19 Hiborough Lane, Oldbury, Westershaw, Lancs, WW3 9GH), *write the circular letter.* You can ignore the reader's address, of course, but start with 'Dear Householder' and a subject heading. You can sign it with your own name as Secretary and Debbie's as co-ordinator. (And your letters will be printed free for you by the mother of one of the group!)

Situation 43: Council house

Your cousin Sophie, and her husband David, Sands have applied for a council house. Their situation is described in Situation 36 on page 65.

The Council has replied, saying that they can be offered a two-bedroom flat within two weeks — but it would be in Grimesthorne, where they do not want to go. One of the reasons is that it would be a long way away from their family, and at least 45 minutes away from David's place of work — very inconvenient if you have to travel by public transport and sometimes have to work nights. However, a major reason is that the shops are too far away for families with small children, and so are the clinics.

The Council cannot offer anything else yet, probably not for another three months at least. But Sophie and David are not interested in the offer at Grimesthorne. *Write to the Housing Manager (Reference HG/56473), at the Town Hall, London Road, Barnsfield BN1 1AA, refusing the offer and explaining why.* Don't sign the letter: leave a space for Sophie or David to sign it.

Situation 44: Letter of application

Some firms do not have application forms for jobs. Maybe the firm is too small for it to be worth their while having forms printed. Sometimes a company prefers to see what you can say about yourself without the help of a form.

Often a firm will say in an advertisement, 'Write, giving full particulars …'. Perhaps it might say, 'Apply in writing (no forms) to …'.

If that is the case, you will need to write a Letter of Application, giving full details of yourself and why you want the job.

As a guide, such letters normally follow this pattern:

1. A short paragraph saying what the job is that you are applying for, and where it was advertised.
2. Details of the qualifications you have that are suitable/applicable to that job. Details of any experience you have.
3. Any details that make you particularly suitable — relevant experience (meeting people, working with others, responsibility, etc.); any special qualifications (Duke of Edinburgh Award, First Aid, driving licence, etc.) and clubs, hobbies and interests. Put down anything that makes you *you* — different from the rest of the crowd!
4. Reasons for wanting this particular job.

Using the job advertisement in Situation 34 on page 64, *write a Letter of Application instead of using a form, using your own details.*